PLANTS & GARDENS

BROOKLYN BOTANIC GARDEN RECORD

BONSAI:
SPECIAL TECHNIQUES

1998

Brooklyn Botanic Garden

STAFF FOR THE ORIGINAL EDITION:

KAN YASHIRODA, GUEST EDITOR

MARY BARNETT, ASSOCIATE EDITOR

STAFF FOR THE REVISED EDITION:

BARBARA B. PESCH, DIRECTOR OF PUBLICATIONS

JANET MARINELLI, ASSOCIATE EDITOR

AND THE EDITORIAL COMMITTEE OF THE BROOKLYN BOTANIC GARDEN

BEKKA LINDSTROM, ART DIRECTOR

JUDITH D. ZUK, PRESIDENT, BROOKLYN BOTANIC GARDEN

ELIZABETH SCHOLTZ, DIRECTOR EMERITUS, BROOKLYN BOTANIC GARDEN

STEPHEN K-M. TIM, VICE PRESIDENT, SCIENCE & PUBLICATIONS

COVER PHOTOGRAPH BY ELVIN MCDONALD
PHOTOGRAPHS BY AUTHORS, EXCEPT WHERE NOTED
DRAWINGS BY EVA MELADY

Plants & Gardens, Brooklyn Botanic Garden Record (ISSN 0362-5850) is published quarterly at 1000 Washington Ave., Brooklyn, N.Y. 11225, by the **Brooklyn Botanic Garden, Inc.** Second-class-postage paid at Brooklyn, N.Y., and at additional mailing offices. Subscription included in Botanic Garden membership dues ($35.00 per year).
Copyright © 1966, 1998 by the Brooklyn Botanic Garden, Inc. PLANTS & GARDENS
ISBN 0-945352-02-6

PLANTS & GARDENS

BROOKLYN BOTANIC GARDEN RECORD

BONSAI:
SPECIAL TECHNIQUES

THIS HANDBOOK IS A REVISED EDITION OF PLANTS & GARDENS, VOL. 22, NO. 2

HANDBOOK #51

Pinus parviflora, Japanese white pine, 267 years old: BBG collection.

Chamaecyparis obtusa 'Nana Gracilis', Hinoki false cypress, BBG collection.

Since the publication of our first handbook on ***Dwarfed Potted Trees — The Bonsai of Japan*** (which has now gone through 38 printings), there has been an ever-increasing interest in this subject in the United States; half a century ago such dwarfed trees were scarcely known outside Japan. Today they have gained world recognition. Indeed, the word "bonsai" has become part of an international vocabulary.

This second bonsai handbook is devoted chiefly to describing methods for the training and culture of some of the more specialized forms of bonsai. Many of the thousands of bonsai questions asked of the Botanic Garden include "How do I create and grow a bonsai forest landscape?", "How can I train a rock-clasping bonsai?", "Are there special techniques for maintaining the truly miniature bonsai?" — and so on. Our earlier

JAPAN

KUNASHIRI ISLAND

HOKKAIDO
formerly EZO

(Ezo Spruce)

(White Pine)
(Zelkova)
(Juniper)

Sendai

Sendai Bay
(Hybrid Pine)

HONSHU

Tokyo

Omiya
(Bonsai Village)

Inland Sea

Mt. Fuji

Yawata

SHIKOKU

Takamatsu
Kinashi Village
(Black and White Pines)

KYUSHU

Mt. Kuju
Mt. Yufu
(Rhododendron kiusianum)

handbook did not answer such questions, at least in any detail, so we went back to Mr. Kan Yashiroda (Guest Editor of two earlier handbooks in the Botanic Garden series) and asked him to take on this new editorial assignment. He invited some of Japan's most talented bonsaimen to participate, and has himself translated their work into English so that we of the West might have access to it.

More than nine thousand students from twenty states have taken popular-level bonsai courses here at the Botanic Garden over the past twenty-five years. Several hundred of them have gone on to our advanced courses. Many worked under Mr. Yashiroda's direction, others under the Garden's own skilled bonsaiman, Mr. Frank Okamura. Their ideas and suggestions are incorporated in short articles throughout the handbook.

Spawned from a knowledge of bonsai culture, the techniques of artistic size-control of trees and shrubs, a pruning for asymmetry, are meeting warm acceptance by discerning gardeners. This is a happy extension of bonsai techniques to the outdoor garden. A noted Japanese author writes that the cult of "the small" has long been a part of the Japanese cultural heritage, due in part to the demands placed upon space by the mountainous terrain of a small and heavily populated island country. Early in Japanese history, patrons of the arts did indeed begin to prize "potted trees," but for centuries these remained trees stunted by nature, occasionally tinkered with but never guided from the start by human craft. The situation is now quite different, and the Western world is privileged to share in this cultural "export" from Japan.

May the two companion Handbooks on Bonsai (we really ought to call them *Bonsai I* and *Bonsai II*) help you on your way to greater understanding and enjoyment of this unique living art. Incidentally, in the BBG series there is a special additional Handbook on this subject for apartment dwellers, *Bonsai for Indoors,* which we should call *Bonsai III*.

– George S. Avery. *Director Emeritus*

EXPERIMENTING WITH BONSAI STYLES

KAN YASHIRODA

Not long ago when some bonsai pictures were shown me by a bonsaiman I know, I asked him if he could claim these as trees that he himself had formed and trained. His answer was in the form of a

KANICHIRO YASHIRODA *is Guest Editor of this handbook. Mr. Yashiroda's home and Acclimatization Garden are located on Shodo Island, in Japan's Inland Sea. (Address: Tonosho-cho, Kagawa Prefecture, Japan). A one-time student gardener at the famous Royal Botanic Gardens at Kew, London, England, Mr. Yashiroda in 1955 and again in 1963 held the C. Stuart Gager Fellowship at the Brooklyn Botanic Garden, where he gave courses in bonsai. He is author of* **Bonsai: Japanese Miniature Trees** *(Faber & Faber, London; Branford, Newton Centre, Mass., 1960). He was Guest Editor of the Brooklyn Botanic Garden's Handbooks on Dwarfed Potted Trees, the Bonsai of Japan (1953), and Japanese Gardens and Miniature Landscapes (1961). In 1955 Mr. Yashiroda received the Botanic Garden's Forsythia Award in recognition of his world-wide plant interests and his interpretation of the horticulture of his native Japan to our Western world.*

protest: He said that no bonsai of note in Japan has been developed by a single man. Rather, it has belonged to many men in the course of years, and each has influenced its training in his own way.

There is much truth in what he said, though his answer had wisely escaped from my question. Bonsai training and culture in Japan are a composite art, just as wood-block printing is a composite art of the painter, engraver and printer.

In Japan many bonsai have been in training since the beginning of the century and are now on the market, most of them at moderate prices. But since a backlog of already-trained bonsai does not exist in the United States, Americans, in their traditional pioneer spirit, must start afresh with nursery stock. Eventually some of you, perhaps some who are beginners today, will create new styles based on American trees and landscapes. While Americans are still learning the art of bonsai culture, however, all the styles which have been developed by the Japanese are available to experiment with.

Although the history of bonsai in Japan can be traced far into the past, the

Ficus aurea bonsai that is only one and a quarter feet high.

styles known as modern were not created until the turn of the century. In the pages that follow, I shall show some examples of modern styles, both standard and unconventional, as well as a few older ones that you might enjoy trying out.

PLANTS USED FOR BONSAI. Turning the pages of Japanese bonsai books, you can see that most of the pictures are of conifers — Japanese white pine, Japanese black pine, Ezo spruce, Chinese juniper and a few others. Among the deciduous trees used are zelkova, Japanese maples, Japanese flowering apricot, pomegranate, Satsuki azaleas, ginkgo and beeches; but this list could go on indefinitely.

The American bonsai grower has no particular trouble obtaining these plants, since many of them are stocked by nurseries in the United States. But in addition there are American trees, and also trees native to other lands, which might make good bonsai material. For example, the natural patterns of growth of long-leaved pines such as the American *Pinus palustris* and the Himalayan pine (*P. wallichiana*) might lead to the creation of a new bonsai style. Both fothergilla in the southeastern United States and Virginia witchhazel (*Hamamelis virginiana*) form lovely flowering bonsai, while shadbush (*Amelanchier*) bonsai have handsome flowers, foliage and fruit. Cotoneasters, which are common now in many countries, have already been so widely adapted as bonsai that a new style based on them seems to be developing. Someday there will be a long list of other plants which have been found suitable for bonsai training.

Making Bonsai Without Wire Coiling

It is possible, and very interesting, to train a plant from nursery shrub to fin-

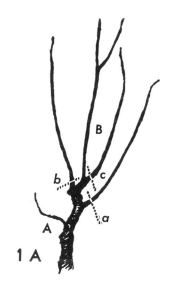

1 A

Pruning cuts
for nursery-grown forsythia.

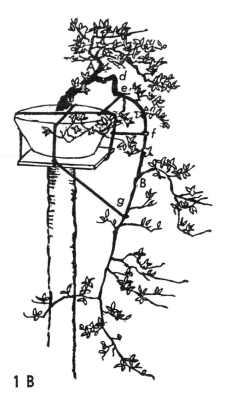

1 B

Training without wire coiling.

ished bonsai without wiring any part of it. Indeed, I firmly believe that the real taste and charm of training bonsai lie in forming them without resorting to wire coiling. Not only are wired branches sometimes unsightly for years, even when the wiring is done by an expert, but the mechanical process may lessen the interest and pleasure of many enthusiasts. It seems to me that this is one of the reasons why the majority of the garden-minded Japanese have no special interest in bonsai. To be generally popular with garden lovers, plants should be trained by more natural methods. But I must admit that this opinion would be opposed by many first-rate bonsaimen — for example, by Saburo Kato, who presents the case in favor of wiring in his article on Ezo spruce (page 70).

In my view, however, one can easily make many deciduous flowering trees and shrubs into bonsai without wire coiling. Only a few guy wires and proper methods of pinching and pruning are necessary. For example, drawing **1A** shows an ordinary forsythia shrub selected from a nursery row. The branches *a, b* and *c* are removed, and it is planted in a container in the autumn. Just before the buds open in the spring, the slender trunk (B) is lowered and fastened by means of guy wires at points *e, f* and *g,* as shown in drawing **1B**. The weaker branch A, which is now at the top, will begin to grow vigorously and form a nicely branched head that can be scissors-trained into some shape such as the one illustrated. In the first year of training, shoots will appear all over the trunk, especially where it is curved downward. Some of these should be rubbed off, and others should be pinched back after they have grown an inch or two so they will branch and re-branch.

If you wish to make a semi-cascade instead of a full one, cut off the trunk at point *f* or a little below it. If you want a slanting-trunked bonsai, remove the trunk somewhere around *d* or *e*. In both cases the drastic pruning will stimulate strong new shoots which will require attention for the first two years of training, since they can spoil the design if they are allowed to grow.

Making Bonsai with Wire Coiling

If you are determined to practice wire coiling in spite of its disadvantages, the most important advice I can give you is that in anything to do with wiring, never be in a hurry. This applies not only to practicing with wire but also to learning the principles of wiring, for it is the hands which must do the learning, slowly and repeatedly, until they can think for you. The novice who grasps the idea in a few minutes and is able to wire a foot long branch in seconds has not mastered — I would almost say, will never master — the technique. I have an old friend who is an expert wire coiler by profession, and whenever he tells me about wiring he is never satisfied until he takes me to a bonsai and, fitting my hand to his, coils wire for a time to show my fingers how to do it. He says this it is the only way he can explain.

Several decades ago M. Makino, an ardent fancier of Satsuki azaleas (*Rhododendron indicum*) who had grown them for twenty years, decided to learn to train them into bonsai. After years of experience, he became the most skillful wire coiler of azaleas of his time. For Americans who are interested in wiring, drawings **2A** and **2B** show examples of his technique.

The azalea in drawing **2A** had been grown in a greenhouse from a cutting for three years and was six feet high. The problem was how to shorten such a very tall plant; if it were made into a twin-trunked bonsai, for example, it would be

2 A

Training with wire coiling: Height of this six-foot azalea has been minimized.

11

2 B

Training with wire coiling:
Azalea wired in one session.

too tall, and its few branches would not fill out the design. By forming it into a cascade as Mr. Makino did, he created an interesting design. He had difficulty in preventing the stems from breaking, however. He warns that wiring which is as extensive as this should be done not all at once, but gradually, from the trunk to a branch and from one branch to the next, with intervals of some months. The whole process might take a year or so; otherwise breakage is likely.

Drawing **2B** shows a Satsuki azalea, variety 'Kwaho', a favorite with azalea growers in Japan. In wiring a plant like this, Mr. Makino generally protects the bark with hemp. He uses no. 10 and no. 15 copper wire for the trunk, coiling so that the spirals are two and a half inches apart. Then he shifts to thinner wire for the branches and places the spirals closer together. Next, protecting his right hand by wrapping it in a towel, he uses it to grasp the foot of the trunk, while he takes hold of the tip with his left hand. Gently and gradually he bends the tree into its main curves. He moves his left hand to the middle of the trunk and bends the minor curves into the lower half. Last, he grips the middle of the trunk with his right hand while with his left curves the upper half.

It is best to do this wiring sometime in the period from late fall to early spring. And unlike the procedure with most plants, the wire should be removed within a year. Otherwise it will cut into the bark, for azaleas are vigorous growers.

Windswept Bonsai

Trees growing on mountaintops, and in other places where constant winds blow, can assume fascinating shapes. It seems to me that this type of bonsai might become a popular style in the United States, though it will probably never be one in Japan because of the disasters regularly inflicted on us by great typhoons. However, Japanese bonsaimen do occasionally create windswept bonsai and windswept forest bonsai as a way of utilizing trees with one-sided branching.

Ezo spruce is a good tree to train in this style, particularly as a forest bonsai. In the windswept forest shown in a drawing **3C**, the tips of trunks *a, b* and *c* have been stripped to reveal the whitish deadwood often seen at the tops of windweathered trees. In this case, where the tips were not as thick as a pencil, the bark was simply peeled away from the wood for a few inches. With thicker treetops, as in the bonsai of drawings **3A** and **3B**, the wood must be worked with a chisel. For example, the branched top of the tree in **3A** was cut off and sharpened, while the top of **3B** was chiseled into a slender deadwood stub. It takes a year or two for these stripped limbs to assume a weathered look so that they appear naturally wind-blasted.

The general rule in windswept design is that nearly all the tree's branches are lowered and trained to grow in one direction, as if from the pressure of the eternal wind. In the case of Ezo spruce, wire training should continue without a break for several years; whenever a branch begins to be constricted, the wire is loosened or removed and replaced with a new one. Sometimes it happens that a branch becomes longer and more vigorous than the others and starts to weaken their growth. This branch can be shortened by shaping it into rippling curves, which enhance the beauty of the design as well as retarding growth and bringing the tree's development back in balance. In windswept compositions the twigs on the branches should not be allowed to sprout densely, for then the fascinating streaming lines of this style will be lost. How to make every twig show the effect of the wind's sculpturing is a pleas-

3 A

3 B

3 C

Windswept designs.
3A: Branched tree-top was cut off and stub was sharpened to appear wind-blasted.
3B: Windswept tree with large chiseled stub.
3C: Windswept forest planting.

13

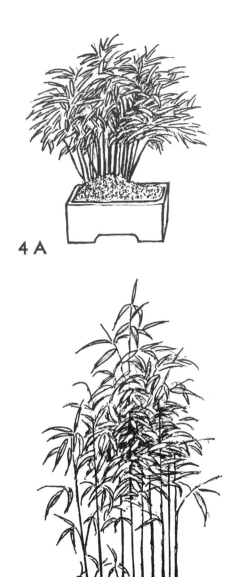

4 A

4 B

4A: Dwarf bamboo —
easiest of the bamboos to grow as
bonsai.
4B: A larger-caned variety.

ant difficulty which adds to the enjoyment of training windswept bonsai.

Bamboo Bonsai

Many American bonsai growers may not know that bamboo thrives as a house plant; indeed, few plants can surpass it as material for indoor bonsai. Besides this point in its favor, the fact that wire is not used in training it pleases those of us who may not care for wiring. Here are directions for making three types of bamboo into bonsai.

1. The easiest bamboos to grow in a container are the very dwarf and hardly varieties such as the one sketched in drawing **4A**. Arundinaria, *Arundinaria chino, A. pygmaea* and some kind of *Sasa* fall in this category. From a bamboo planting in a garden, carefully dig up a handful of slender canes in early spring before the new shoots come out. Plant them in a container and trim them well, either shortening them considerably or cutting them back to the ground. After potting, water them until they are saturated. In early summer, cut off the leaves so that smaller new leaves will form. Every spring when the new shoots appear, thin out some of the older plants to preserve the balance of the arrangement.

2. In the case of thicker-caned bamboo — *Arundinaria hindsii, Phyllostachys bambusoides* and *P. nigra* — as shown in drawing **4B**, first find some comparatively shallow-growing stems with promising buds. You might discover a very small already-formed plant in an oriental shop. In colder climates, plant in a protected coldframe for the first winter, and in spring when the shoots have grown a few inches, dig up the whole plant, wash the soil off the roots and replant in the ground. This will considerably reduce the size

14

of the new growth. If growth is still too strong, decrease the amount of water and sunlight the plants receive. In early summer, cut off the leaves to develop smaller new leaves, and the plant is then ready to pot as a bonsai which can be enjoyed immediately.

3. The thickest-caned of the bamboos, tortoise-shell bamboo (*Phyllostachys heterocycla*), is a very interesting one to train (and is edible, incidentally). Propagation is by the method described in the preceding paragraph, except that when the young shoots are a few inches high, their sheaths should be peeled off as each new leaf appears. This process reduces the distance between nodes, inhibits growth and helps to dwarf the plant.

Fruit-Tree Bonsai

A good fruit-tree bonsai, bearing a few fruits and placed as decoration in the living room or an alcove, has a refined tastefulness which makes this a most desirable bonsai type. Since it takes time to create such a planting from the regular one- to three-year-old nursery stock grown for orchards, I recommend that you look for old fruit trees which have passed their age limit but are still healthy at the base. Or a plant such as a small-leaved orange tree which has been grown for years as a house plant can be repotted and retrained as a bonsai.

As an example of the use of old fruit trees, the bonsai grower who finds a pomegranate tree with decayed heartwood and only a thin layer of living wood can saw it off two to three feet above the ground. If all the thick roots are cut back close to the trunk, it can be grown successfully in a container with no more than the usual care. Young shoots will spring up vigorously, and from them a few should be selected for training. This procedure is also frequently used with

5 A

5 B

5A: Semi-cascade bonsai made from an orange tree which had been a house plant.
5B: Persimmon bonsai created by pruning a full-sized tree back to its lowest limb.

15

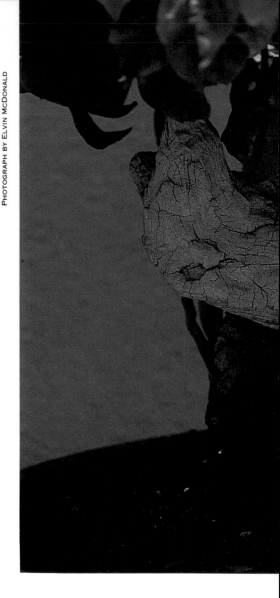

PHOTOGRAPH BY ELVIN MCDONALD

Japanese apricot, and to a lesser degree with the other rosaceous fruit trees. All are beautiful as flowering bonsai, and they can be induced to fruit. Choose types with small-sized fruits , however.

An orange tree with small leaves which has been grown as a house plant can easily be made into one of several bonsai styles. To create the semi-cascade shown in drawing **5A**, the unnecessary branches were pruned away and the tree was planted in the container at a slant. After it was settled and growing well, the trunk and branches were curved by wiring. Although orange trees are not difficult to wire, their bark is easily damaged and should be wrapped with cloth before the wire coiling is begun. The

Trunk detail of *Bougainvillea* 'Barbara Karst' in training for eight years
by Harry Iba.

weak **A** branch shown in the illustration will grow sturdily now that it has been brought into an upright position, for one characteristic of orange trees is that the top growth is strong.

Persimmon trees make colorful bonsai with deep orange-red fruit and flaming autumn tints. When a suitable tree is found, often it can be given its main shape as a bonsai simply by cutting it back to the lowest limb. Sometimes, as shown in drawing **5B**, a stub of the trunk is left on as a picturesque feature, since this is the way trees in orchards are frequently pruned. Further training with wire must be done carefully because of the brittleness of persimmon branches.

Twin-Trunked Bonsai

As drawings **6A** and **6B** show, there are two kinds of twin-trunked bonsai: a pair of trees planted so close together that they seem like one, and a single tree whose trunk forks near the ground. Twin-trunked bonsai have a less grand and dignified appearance than the formal single-trunked bonsai which the Japanese admire so much. They are easier and quicker to make, however, and are so interesting to design that the owner learns many principles of bonsai while he amuses himself in training them.

Whenever we come to select potential bonsai from nursery rows, we find only a few that are desirable for orthodox single upright trees. If we look again at the others, however, we discover some that will make nice twin-trunked arrangements. When choosing trees to plant as a pair, find two that combine well not only in branches but also in their root systems; roots which lie on the surface should not cross each other, for example, and the root systems of both trees should be approximately equal in size and vigor.

Then, as you would with any bonsai, thin and shorten the roots and branches of the two trees and plant them together in a container.

Train two-tree bonsai by wire coiling — in this case, a thorough wiring which involves every branch. Forming the overall shape is relatively easy, and so absorbing that you may find you have overwired. With these bonsai, however, excessive wiring is not so objectionable or injurious to the tree, particularly if one takes care to coil the wire evenly and use the proper wire sizes. In positioning the branches, remember that the foliage should be arranged to give snatchy views of the two trunks all the way to the top. The branches of conifers are generally lowered, while those of deciduous trees

6 A

6 B

Twin-trunked bonsai.
6A: A pair of trees planted close together. Hinoki cypress,
Ezo spruce, cryptomeria and other delicate-foliaged varieties are suited to this style.
6B: A single Japanese white pine with forked trunk.

are wired to grow either horizontally or upward, depending on how the mature specimens appear in nature.

The tree in drawing **6B**, a dense forked-trunk pine bonsai that has become a favorite in Japan, is shaped by considerably less wiring than a two-tree composition. After a few years of basic wire coiling to arrange the main branches, it can be trained entirely by selective pinching of the new growth and occasional thinning of the branches to allow more sunlight to filter deep into the tree. While the wire is still being used, be careful that it does not constrict the branches.

Three-Trunked Bonsai

Between single-tree bonsai and forest bonsai lies the charming arrangement of three-trunked bonsai. This composition presents slightly different problems of design and culture from the other styles, although some bonsaimen consider it a version of forest bonsai.

Drawings **7A** and **7B** illustrate other three-trunked designs — a modern one in A and an older version in B. The three slender-trunked pines in **7B** are too thin to use as single bonsai, but they make an appealing arrangement when planted very close together. In **7A**, each tree not only contributes to the design of the whole, but has an individual beauty as well. The closely integrated relationship between the trees is the important element in both designs and should be the central concern in their training. In addition, since there will inevitably be a struggle for survival among trees in such a small container, the bonsai grower must know which tree is the weakest so that he can give it extra care. Because the trees are so intimately related, these compositions are not simple to re-form if one of the plants dies.

The individual trees in a three-trunked bonsai are larger than those in a

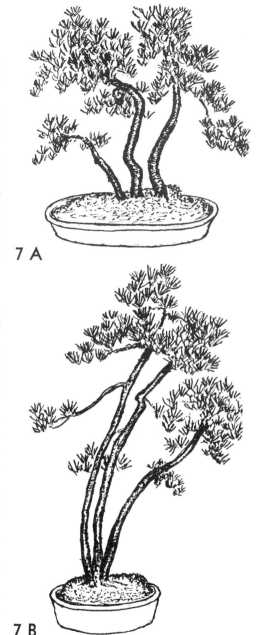

7 A

7 B

Three-trunked bonsai.
7A: Modern version.
7B: An earlier style, in which trees are too slender to use as single bonsai. Japanese white pine is well suited for both versions.

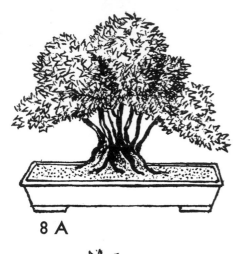

8 A

8 B

8A: Modern version of clustered maples.

8B: Earlier clustered style, appropriate for birches, beeches and other slender-trunked trees.

miniature forest, and the roots are not easy to establish in a shallow container. Plants should be used which can be made to produce good fibrous roots by means of root pruning. Japanese white pine is particularly suited to three-trunked bonsai, since it responds well to root pruning, pinching and wiring.

Generally, trees of the size used in three-trunked plantings produce exceptionally long and strong roots growing around the inside edge of the container. To reduce these, take hold of one or two of the trees and lift the plant out of the container; the ball of the soil usually comes out easily. Then prune the long roots drastically — or remove them completely if you judge that the plant has enough shorter roots to survive — and replace the planting as it is. In reality, this is a quick partial repotting procedure. Add more soil mixture to the container before replacing the root ball.

Clustered Bonsai

Of the clustered plantings in **8A** and **8B**, A is a modern style, B an older one. I like both equally well and recommend that both be tried out with small nursery stock.

To make a planting like **8A** from Japanese maple seedlings, group seedlings which are 12 or more inches high close together in an ordinary deep flowerpot. Keep them there one, two or even more years, meanwhile pinching and pruning them and cutting back the tops to give them a symmetrical shape. When the main roots are thick and deep enough, move the clump to a shallow container, exposing the tops of the roots as shown. If the weather at that time is dry and windy, protect the exposed roots at first with moistened sphagnum moss. Since maples are very breakable except for the young shoots, be careful about wiring, especially toward the nodes. Pinch back the new shoots every spring to induce denser foliage. Although (as with all bonsai) it is desirable to use varieties with small leaves, dwarf maples are not appropriate for cluster plantings, because their growth is too dense and shrublike.

Among the suggestions I have given here, some of them easy for a novice, some technically more demanding, some traditional in Japanese bonsai design and some quite free and informal, I hope everyone can find a few styles he would like to experiment with. In Japan, bonsai styles have not remained fixed in recent years: since World War II, flowering bonsai have become more popular, the number of "light" designs as opposed to formal, balanced compositions has increased, and the overwhelming preponderance of the conifers has somewhat moderated. As styles which are distinctively American begin to be developed by growers in the United States, Japanese bonsai fashions may come to respond to influences from the West even as Japan's styles have influenced western designs. 🌿

PHOTOGRAPH BY ELVIN MCDONALD

Juniperus chinensis 'Sargentii' and
J. occidentalis,
considered to be 1000 years old,
19 years in training

STONE-CLASPING BONSAI

SEIZAN ITO

The objective in creating a stone-clasping bonsai is to reproduce in a container the effect of a mountain landscape with bold cliffs and steep ravines. In the version of this style now fashionable in Japan, the tree is subordinated to the rock, whose shape and color are the features emphasized for appreciation. The plants, which should be low-growing, with exposed heavy roots, are placed as appendages to the top or side of the stones, as in the multiple-tree rock planting below.

In other versions of stone-clasping bonsai, which are shown on the following pages, the stone is an accessory to the tree. For example, the bonsai seems to hold a stone at its foot, or its roots are trained over a stone so that their formation can be appreciated.

As with forest bonsai, the loveliness of stone-clasping bonsai lies in their presentation, in miniature, of scenes copied from nature. They should convey the feeling of a grand view of a mountaintop, or an islet in our Inland Sea. Just as a painting reproduces a natural landscape, so the scenery of seabeach, islet or perpendicular cliff can be re-created with living plants in a small container.

Advantages of Stone-Clasping Bonsai

- Young trees can be used, and so can "defective" trees which would not make good formal upright bonsai. Thus a fine stone-clasping bonsai often can be created from ordinary plants.

- A bonsai which has a finished look can be made in a short time. Then as the planting ages, it becomes even more attractive.

- Stone-clasping bonsai are easy to create; a novice can soon learn to make an interesting one. They are also easy to remake if the tree grows out of scale or the owner decides to change the design.

SEIZAN ITO *is a member of the Osaka (Japan) Bonsai Club, and a professional bonsai nurseryman and landscape architect.*

Selecting the Stone

When looking for stones to use in this kind of planting, remember that rugged, jagged and oddly shaped ones are best for evoking the grandeur of a wild landscape. Choose rocks from a mountainside rather than from the bed of a river, where they will have been smoothed by the water's action. However, the base of the stone must be stable; a tree planted on a teetering rock will not grow properly, if at all. If the bottom is not already flat, it should be worked in order to form a steady base. Another practical consideration is the weight of the rock; do not choose one which is too heavy to carry unless the finished bonsai will have a permanent location.

Besides valuing picturesque shapes, the Japanese appreciate stones which contain different colors and textures. A cascade stone, for example, has a smooth white streak down it that gives the effect of a mountain waterfall. Other stones with white outcroppings can be used to suggest winter landscapes. In addition to such scenic effects, the colors of variegated

Trees are subordinated to the stone: A multiple-tree bonsai. These trees are small in relation to the pinnacled rock.

stones are lovely in themselves and set off the colors of the trees planted on them.

Although it should possess some of the dramatic features suggested here, a rock for a stone-clasping bonsai need not be perfect. A stone with several good points can be used effectively even if it also has an ugly face, for this can be concealed by well-placed plantings. The stone-clasping bonsai pictured on these pages will give some idea of the many shapes and types of stones that can be planted to create miniature landscapes.

Plants for Stone-Clasping Bonsai

As with all bonsai materials, plants chosen for stone-clasping bonsai should have small leaves. This is especially important when the planting is meant to suggest a faraway scene. Among the more desirable specimens are Ezo spruce, Japanese white pine, Chinese or similar kinds of

23

Juniperus chinensis 'San Jose' has been trained for seven years by Kaz Yoneda.

juniper, and small-leaved rhododendrons and azaleas.

In addition to the main tree or trees, stone-clasping bonsai often include mosses and other creeping plants which have small shapely leaves. Dwarf ivies and dwarf woody plants such as *Rhododendron serpyllifolium* can also be used as secondary plantings.

How to Fasten the Tree Completely to the Stone

To create the version of stone-clasping bonsai in which the tree is subordinated to the stone, fasten the bonsai to the face of a comparatively large rock by the steps given below. The mass of soil placed around the tree roots (as in the cross section shown in drawing E) is all the soil the tree will ever have, and it is necessary to use a special mixture.

SEASON. Although early spring (just before growth normally starts) is the best season for making this type of bonsai, some species can be planted and trained at other seasons. If planted in summer, the tree must be carefully shaded until it becomes settled on the stone; if in winter, it must be protected from freezing weather.

SOIL. The soil in this type of planting must have enough fibrous substance to hold it together, yet enough clay-like material to stick to the sides of a stone and to retain moisture. Japanese bonsaimen use a mixture of powdered mountain moss, powdered blackish and reddish clay, and *Ketozuchi*, a soil formed in lakes and marshes from the decay of organic matter.

Inasmuch as these special materials are not available outside Japan, each grower will need to experiment with soils in his locality. One possibility is to combine two parts clay, one part finely screened peat moss, and a small amount of some shredded material such as dried sugarcane fiber (Stayz-Dri), dried shredded cornstalks, or fine nylon string cut into one-half- to one-inch lengths. Before it is spread on the stone, the mixture should be formed into a paste by adding a little water and stirring thoroughly. If the paste does not adhere well to the stone, more clay can be added to the first layer of soil which will be spread on the rock surface.

STEPS IN PLANTING. Soil, tree and moss are attached to the stone by the following methods:

1. Select a position for the tree where it will not conceal the good features of the rock. Using an adhesive such as epoxy cement, glue a few rings made of slender copper wire around the spot chosen. See drawing C for examples of ring placement in three possible tree positions. The rings should be about one-half inch in diameter and can be shaped in any of the ways shown in drawing B. After the glue has hardened, tie very slender copper wire to the rings as illustrated in drawing D.

2. Prepare the soil mixture described above, then moisten it to a paste and spread it a half inch thick over the area on the rock where the tree is to be planted. (Add more clay if the soil will not stick to the stone.)

3. Unpot the tree and gently shake or wash off all the soil attached to its roots. Do not prune the roots; rather, spread and press them lightly into the soil mixture on the rock. If they seem to be drying out as you work, spray lightly with a fine mist.

4. Fasten the roots with the very slender wire as shown in the cross-section sketch of E. Notice that a thin piece of

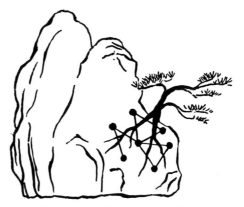

A. The general idea: As sketched here without soil and moss layers, tree roots are laced to rock with wires passed through rings. Circles represent rings glued to the stone.

B. Rings of half-inch diameter can be shaped in any of these forms.

C. Copper wire rings glued to stone in three possible tree positions.

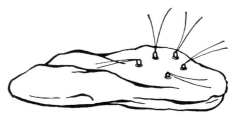

D. Very slender copper wire is tied to rings after glue has hardened.

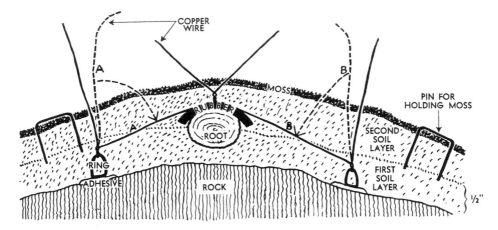

E. Sectional diagram showing root in relation to soil layers; note how wires hold it in position.

rubber is placed where root and wire come into contact, in order to prevent damage to the root. The general idea of fastening the roots with wire is illustrated in A, where the circles represent the rings glued to the stone.

5. After the roots have been fastened, spread a second layer of the soil mixture on top of them. Also apply soil to areas where the roots will reach in the future. Use enough of the mixture for the tree to grow in; remember that this is all the soil the plant will have.

6. Cover the soil with a low-growing or creeping moss. To do this, use a knife to scrape away all excess earth from the underside of the moss mat. Apply a thin coating of finely powdered loam to the scraped underside, spray it lightly with water, and turn the moss over and press it into the soil of the rock planting. Sometimes several kinds of moss are blended together. Occasionally underplantings of herbaceous species are used instead of moss.

7. Since the main role of the mosses is to prevent the soil mixture from washing away, they should be firmly attached to the soil. For this purpose, make U-shaped pins from slender copper wire and use them to fasten the moss as shown in drawing E. Be sure the pins are long enough to hold, and insert enough of them at different angles and in different places to make the planting secure.

8. Water the bonsai thoroughly with a fine spray.

A Tree Planted in a Hole in the Stone

As shown in the drawing above, bonsai made by this method look as if they had been planted using the techniques listed in the previous section, but actually they grow like trees in containers. The holes they are planted in, which can be made with a drill by a stonemason or stone monument maker, should extend through the stone to the bottom. Their diameter is usually about two to four inches, although some large plantings in outsize stones may require larger holes.

Planting procedures resemble those

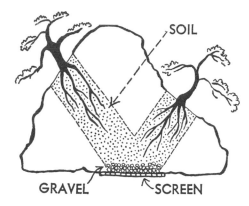

SOIL

GRAVEL SCREEN

Trees planted in holes drilled through the stone appear to be stone-clasping bonsai, but care is the same as for bonsai in containers.

for regular bonsai. Copper mesh is glued across the bottom of the hole, a drainage layer of gravel is added, and regular bonsai soil (*not* the special stone-clasping mixture) is used. As with bonsai in traditional containers, the trees are periodically removed for root pruning and then replanted with some fresh soil.

Training Roots Over a Stone and Into Soil

In this version, the tree is planted with the main roots astride a stone, as if it were on horseback. The rock is set into a shallow container, and the roots are led down into soil.

As this kind of planting ages, the gnarled and twisting roots themselves become one of its beautiful features. In following their own style of growth and accommodating themselves to the shape of the stone, the roots of every tree form individual patterns.

Techniques for fastening a tree to a stone, and for protecting the roots until they are well established, are given elsewhere.

Care of Stone-Clasping Bonsai

● WATERING: Since these plantings dry out more quickly than bonsai in containers, they usually need at least one extra watering on sunny days. In all weather they should be watched closely to prevent excessive dryness; frequent watering is the most important single element in the care of stone-clasping bonsai.

● FERTILIZING: Instead of manure, which is difficult to apply evenly to rock plantings, weak liquid manure or other liquid fertilizer should be given several times during the growing season.

● REPLACING SOIL: Trees which are growing exclusively on the stone are never repotted or root-pruned. Instead, the moss is lifted off every few years and additional stone-clasping mixture is spread on the roots to replace soil washed away by watering. My experience with a variety of Ezo spruce called 'Yatsufusa' has been that the trees develop faster when planted on a stone rather than in a container, but that growth becomes poor after a decade or more, owing to the prolonged scarcity of soil. Then I find I must move the tree to a container to recover, while I plant a younger one in its place. Perhaps other species may need the same treatment after they have spent many years on a stone.

● REPOTTING: For trees which are trained over a stone and into soil, the soil in the container is renewed periodically, as in the case of ordinary bonsai. The tree should never be separated from the rock, however; tree and stone are gently tapped out of the container together, and the roots which were growing in the soil are pruned in the regular manner. Fresh soil is added to the container, and tree and stone are set back into it as a unit.

27

Pinus thunbergii, Japanese black pine, 22 years old,
in training for 20 years by Eddy Harata.

FOREST BONSAI

SEIZAN ITO

I n a forest bonsai a number of trees are arranged in a container so that they suggest a woodland scene — for example, a view of deep forest, woods on a seacoast or a plain fringed with scattered groves. Like stone-clasping bonsai, forest plantings have immense variety in subject matter. They can show close-ups or faraway perspectives, young forest or old, dense growth or sparse wind-battered trees; there seems no end to the effects which can be produced in this free and informal bonsai style.

Trees set haphazardly into a container, however, will not give the illusion of a natural landscape, no matter what scene is being created. Because it is a work of art made with living plants, a forest bonsai requires the same attention to composition that one finds in a good painting. Ultimately it must suggest not only the appearance but the mood of a forest; it cannot be called a fine bonsai unless one can almost hear a birdsong from its interior, or the sound of a running brook.

In Japan, even such a forest masterpiece is less expensive than a single tree in the traditional formal upright style, because the materials used in forest plantings are relatively low in price. Trees which have impressive trunks, evenly developed spread of roots, and correct branching required for orthodox single bonsai are rare and costly. Bonsai nurserymen often refer to other trees which do not meet such rigorous standards as "materials for forest bonsai." These less-than-perfect trees show an in-dividuality which can contribute to the special charm and grace of forest plantings. A fine forest created by an expert bonsaiman has a poetic quality which reflects his feeling for the loveliness of nature as well as his great technical skill. Such a man will sort through scores or even hundreds of trees to find five or ten for his forest scene.

Advantages of Forest Bonsai

Besides the great advantage that less-than-perfect trees can be made into attractive forests, plants too young to have ornamental value as single bonsai can also be used. It depends mainly on the skill with which they are arranged. And although trees in the formal upright style take thirty to fifty (or with some species, even a hundred) years to become finished bonsai, it is possible to compose a forest that can be appreciated and enjoyed immediately. If the materials are already assembled and the design has been planned and sketched beforehand, the bonsai can be made in one sitting.

Larix kaempferi, Japanese Larch, is 15 years old, in training 13 years.

With the passage of time, a forest bonsai, like a stone-clasping one, becomes increasingly harmonious and well composed. After years of cultivation and training, it has a charm quite different from the poised dignity of a single fine bonsai. Because of the informality of this style, a forest bonsai can easily be recomposed if part of it is damaged or becomes weakened in growth. Sometimes changing the position of only one tree is enough to form a new design.

It is possible for beginners, especially those with some experience in art, to create most pleasing arrangements in this style. And since inexpensive plant materials can be used, beginners can experiment freely in order to develop skill with forest composition.

Plants for Forest Bonsai

In selecting plants for forest arrangements, bonsaimen prefer certain characteristics that may be found in many species, both evergreen and deciduous:

- As with all bonsai, small-leaved trees should be used in a forest planting.

- Because most forest containers are very shallow, species which take kindly to severe root pruning are best.

- Ideally, all trees in a forest should be of the same clone — that is, propagated from the same parent plant. Their identical growth habits make the bonsai easier to care for and more unified in appearance.

- It is rewarding to use trees whose new sprouts characteristically are lighter in color than the older growth. The foliage then provides exquisite color contrasts during the growing season.

The most suitable forest species are Ezo spruce, cryptomeria, Hinoki cypress and needle juniper among the conifers; and beeches, hornbeams, maples and zelkovas among deciduous trees.

Both for appearance and for the health of the plants, it is best to use only one kind of tree in a forest. Occasionally a good forest bonsai contains a mixed planting, but in order to avoid a garish effect the designer is careful to make one species dominate the composition; he uses only a few of the second kind as accents. Even so, the different rates of growth of the two species sooner or later destroy the balance of the arrangement; the stronger variety tends to dominate or starve out the weaker.

Containers

In general, the container should be very shallow to add to the feeling that the forest is tall and spacious. Shallow oval or oblong containers are well suited for most forest plantings, though slender-trunked trees arranged in a strip, such as Ezo spruces are, look best in shallow rectangular ones. Flattish, often slightly concave stones also make excellent containers because they contribute to the "natural" character of the planting. In Japan such stones from Kurama, Kyoto, are greatly prized.

Soil and Season

Since regular bonsai soil is used in forest plantings, whatever mixture has been satisfactory for growing a single bonsai can be duplicated in a forest made from the same species. As for the best season to create a forest, it is the same as the best season for planting and transplanting all bonsai: early spring just before the buds begin to open. At this period the severe root pruning often needed because of the shallow containers is less likely to kill the trees. Forests can also be made at some other times of year if only moderate root pruning is required; but midsummer and midwinter are to be avoided.

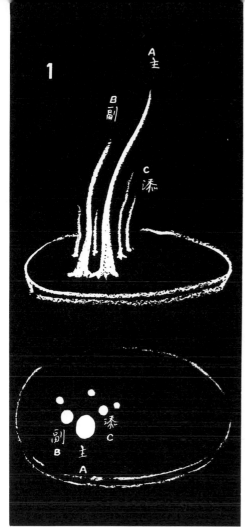

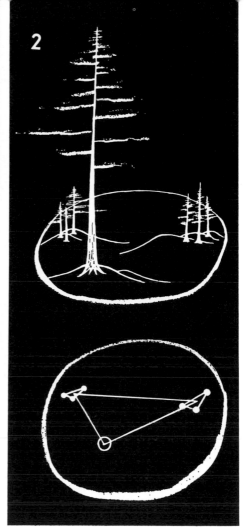

A forest family,
with trees A, B and C,
the grandparents and parents,
serving as the focal points.

Front elevation and ground plan using
uneven triangles to create irregularity
and depth. Perspective is emphasized
by mounding the soil into tiny hills.

The Design

The overall design of a bonsai forest
comes from the arrangement and varying sizes of the trees; the general principles behind the design are the same as
those for the composition of a painting
or a piece of sculpture. Bonsai growers
who have had no training in art will
learn these principles as they experiment

with group plantings and see which ones
take on the appearance of a natural landscape. Here are a few guiding suggestions:

- In general, an odd number of trees is
  used in each small cluster within the
  arrangement, as well as in the planting as a whole. This helps avoid sym-
  metry and gives the random appearance of a natural forest.

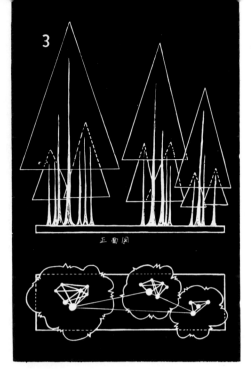

Front elevation and ground plan for a straight-trunked forest bonsai. Suitable for use with Ezo spruce, cryptomeria, needle juniper and other conifers.

- Just as a family consists of parents, grandparents and children, so a forest bonsai has a main tree and a secondary main tree around which the less important trees are grouped like children, as in drawing 1. The arrangement should have a family feeling of unity and harmony.
- One commonly used ground plan is an uneven triangle with the three main trees at its vertexes, and with the other trees forming smaller triangles around these. The sketches in drawings 2, 3 and 4 show the idea. Such an organization results in fairly definite clusters of trees and a focal point that is off-center. This can help create the impression of irregularity and depth given by an actual landscape.
- Trees that are branched thickly on only one side are usually placed at the sides of the arrangement, and those with low branches are often planted at the back.
- In some compositions, particularly in large containers, the soil can be graded to give the appearance of a hilly surface.
- The grower should develop an awareness of line, of form, of the shapes of the individual trees and the curves of

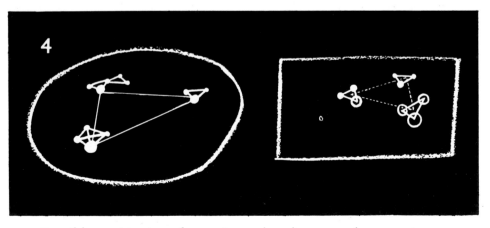

Possible positioning of trees in oval and rectangular containers.

Fagus crenata, beech forest, in bonsai show in Osaka, 1980.

their trunks and branches. Selecting some of these lines to carry through the composition, echoing and varying them from branch to branch and tree to tree — these are skills which the beginner develops as he experiments, and which can be seen at their highest in the truly great forest bonsai.

- As with all compositions in the visual arts, the empty spaces are as important as the arrangement of trees. Learn to notice the different ways in which forest bonsai use space.

- Since the source of music, painting and all the arts is nature, we should copy natural landscapes, learn from them and come to be humble. As the painter fills his sketchbook with forms which catch the eye, so we bonsaimen should sketch and photograph impressive scenery, going out often to view field and mountain.

Making a Forest from Separate Trees

Here is the method used in Japan for planting a forest from separate trees. (If you wish instead to create a forest from a single tree trunk laid down on the soil, see pages 36 and 37 which follow this article.)

1. SKETCH THE DESIGN. After studying each tree and deciding how to arrange a forest scene, it is best to draw a ground plan and a sketch of the front view, like the plans shown on these pages. Not only do drawings help in working out the design, but they save confusion in planting. If the composition is a large one with many trees, it may be desirable to sketch the side views as well.

2. PREPARE THE CONTAINER. As for all bonsai containers, cover the bottom holes with plastic screening. Put down a thin layer of gravel for drainage and a thin layer of bonsai soil on top of it.

3. PRUNE ROOTS AND BRANCHES. If the trees are potted, unpot them, shake away excess soil and cut back any long roots in order to create a compact root system. If some trees have only a few roots which are too large for the shallow container, they may be cut halfway through with a razor blade in one or more places and bent to conform to the soil space available. If much of a tree's root system is removed, then the top must be correspondingly reduced.

4. PLANT TREES. Plant the first few trees in order of size, i.e., the main tree, the secondary main tree and so on. Then, as with any bonsai, firm the soil by jabbing with a chopstick so the dry soil will fall into any air pockets remaining around the roots.
IF TREES WILL NOT STAY IN PLACE: Sometimes it is difficult to position the trees; each as it is planted pushes the others askew so that they do not conform to the plan. For this problem different bonsaimen prefer different solutions:

● As each tree is being planted, some growers wet the soil heaped around it to a sticky consistency. This alone may be enough to hold a tree in place.

Wire through drain holes of container can be used to fasten trees in place.

Trees can be held in position by tying with string, which is passed around and knotted underneath the container.

- Others prop the tree into position with pieces of moistened moss placed at the foot of the trunks.
- When the container is being prepared (step 2), wires can be threaded through the bottom holes before the gravel is spread, as shown in drawing A. Then while the trees are being planted, the wires are tied around the root balls to fasten them in position.
- The trees can be tied to the container with strings by the method shown in drawing B. At about the time when the roots begin to take hold, the strings rot away.

5. CARE AND TRAINING. Immediately after planting, the forest should be watered with a fine spray until water runs out of the drain holes in the container. Place in shade, and shelter from wind and rain until new growth has started.

After a few weeks to a month or more, new fibrous roots will have formed and the trees will be securely anchored. Training, whether by wiring or by pruning alone, can then be started.

In about two years, when the container is crowded with roots, the forest is unpotted and root-pruned as a unit. Damaged trees or trees that have become too dominant are replaced, and the forest is replanted with the addition of some fresh soil.

A
FOREST
FROM A SINGLE TREE

One of the most easily mastered techniques, offering no particular difficulties for a novice, is the raising of a forest from a single growing tree. Such a forest, being uniform in character throughout, takes on autumn color simultaneously and is simpler to plant than forests composed of separate trees. There are two ways of making single-tree forests. The first, which is described below, is commonly used with deciduous trees. The second, given on the opposite page, is best for evergreens.

— *Kan Yashiroda*

USING A DECIDUOUS TREE

❶ **SELECTING A TREE**: In early spring select a deciduous tree (such as Japanese maple, zelkova or carpinus) with numerous dormant buds. It is preferable to use a tree which has one or two main branches near the base. In general, the more branches the tree has, the more treelets there will be in the future forest.

❷ **PREPARING THE CONTAINER:** Prepare the container as for any bonsai (for example, see step 2, page 35).

❸ **PRUNING**: Prune the trunk and branches severely; when the tree is laid down, it should not be close to the edges of the container at any point.

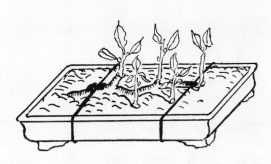

Left: In early spring, select a deciduous tree with numerous dormant buds.

Right: When a tree is pruned back to a single bud on each branch and laid down on the soil in a container, vigorous shoots develop.

❹ PLANTING: Lay the tree flat on the soil, remove any roots which tend to point upward, and cover the remaining roots with more bonsai soil. It is customary to place the roots at the left of the container. Bury the trunk and branches up to half or two-thirds of their diameter.

❺ **Securing the tree**: Fasten the tree in position with wires either threaded through the drainage holes or wrapped around the outside of the container, as shown in the right-hand drawing above. Notice that pieces of rubber are used to protect the tree wherever the wire would touch it.

❻ WATERING: Water thoroughly, and keep the trunk and roots covered with moist sphagnum moss until the dormant buds start to grow.

❼ TRAINING: When the new shoots are several inches high, select those in the most pleasing positions for training, and remove the others. To create tapering trunks, pinch each shoot back to one of the lower buds, and repeat this procedure as new shoots develop from the dormant buds throughout the growing season.

— ADAPTED FROM KAN YASHIRODA, ***BONSAI: JAPANESE MINIATURE TREES*** (BRANFORD).

Using an Evergreen

❶ DRAWINGS A AND B: In early spring when growth is starting, unwanted branches are pruned from an evergreen tree. It is then laid on its side in a box and fastened tightly so that it can be wired with reasonable

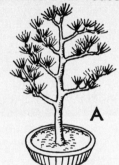

Pruned evergreen, early spring.

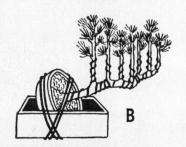

Tree lashed on side, branches wired to grow upward.

ease. All the branches are wired to grow in the same direction, and the trunk is wire-shaped to give it pleasing undulations. Further shaping of the branches, which now represent small upright trees, can best be carried out in future years during the spring growth period.

❷ Drawing C: The container is prepared by placing screening over the bottom holes, threading wire through them, and adding a layer of gravel and a layer of bonsai soil. The size of the tree's root ball is reduced, and any roots that would form too much of a hump in the shallow container are removed completely. Laid flat on the soil, the tree trunk is tied firmly in place with the wires which have been passed through holes in the container. Drawing C provides an "X-ray view" through the soil and gravel to show how the anchoring wires hold the tree. Strips of leather or rubber are used to protect the bark from being cut by the wire. The dotted lines beneath the center hole in the drawing illustrate how the wire which has been threaded through this hole is anchored underneath the container by a short piece of stick or heavy wire.

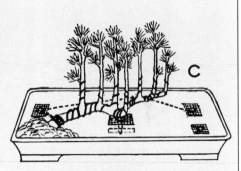

Transplanted tree: "X-ray view" through soil to show how wires hold it in container.

❸ **DRAWING D**: The final step is to partially bury the horizontal trunk by adding more bonsai soil. The container is then set in a place which receives strong light but is protected from direct sun, rain and wind. It should not be moved or disturbed in any way for several months so that the branches may be enticed to send forth roots.

— ADAPTED FROM TOSHIO KAWAMOTO AND JOSEPH Y. KURIHARA, **BONSAI-SAIKEI** (NIPPON SAIKEI CO., TOKYO).

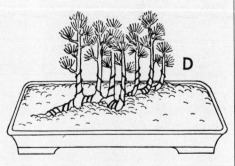

Final step: Tree with trunk partially buried in soil.

A TRADITION OF BONSAI AMATEURS

MAKOTO INAWASHIRO

Since the sixteenth century, when a great feudal lord then ruling this territory began to encourage the growing of bonsai, Sendai has been a focus for bonsai art in Japan. The lord was interested in bonsai (as well as in Noh plays, painting, Waka poems, and tea ceremony) as a pursuit for educated and cultivated men, and this approach to the art has been continued in Sendai by a succession of distinguished amateurs. A famous bonsai connoisseur early in this century was Nobukana Kajiya, a railroad executive who admired bonsai grown

from seed. He believed that these are the only true bonsai, and he became an almost violent advocate of this point of view in Japanese bonsai circles. Another skillful amateur of the same period, Misuke Tanzawa, was a college president, and two Sendai judges became prominent bonsai growers. Today many fine bonsai trained by these men are seen on the shelves of connoisseurs in Sendai.

The trident maple (*Acer buergerianum*) shown at the right was grown from a seed planted in 1879 by another outstanding amateur, Makoto Matsukara, the first major of Sendai. He and his son, who helped him train it, presented it to me about twenty-five years ago. A splendid

MAKOTO INAWASHIRO *is President of the Miyagi Sekei Bonsai Society in Sendai, Japan.*

Maple bonsai shown here in autumnal garb.

healthy tree, it is known for its shapely leaves in spring and deep crimson color in autumn. The following bonsai techniques are the ones I have found best to keep it healthy and preserve its beauty.

Every spring before the buds open, I transplant the tree, removing it from the container and reducing the size of the ball of soil at the same time that I cut back the roots. I cover the drain holes of the container with fine screening, spread a thin layer of coarse sand for good drainage, and put down a layer of compost prepared with three parts of sand to seven parts of a red and black clay-loam mixture. Then I place the tree in the container and tamp more compost around it,

taking care that the roots everywhere come in contact with the soil. For ten days after this, the tree stays in shade, and after two weeks I give it fertilizer.

In early summer I pinch all the leaves off the tree, and smaller new leaves, lovely as emeralds, come out to replace them. (This technique, incidentally, can also be used with hornbeams, zelkovas, ginkgo and a few other deciduous trees. Removal of all their leaves not only results in a second crop of smaller leaves and stimulates brighter autumn color, but with younger trees, it hastens their development as bonsai. All leaves must never be removed from conifers, however; instead, their young sprouts are simply pinched back).

When the maple bonsai given me by the Matsukuras drops its leaves in late autumn, I bring it into the house for appreciation as frequently as I can without interrupting its dormancy. To me, the real beauty of deciduous trees is in the naked state of their winter-bare branches. One of the privileges we have as bonsai growers is that we can experience the great transitions of nature through seasonal changes in the miniature trees which are so close to us.

In Sendai we are fortunate in the natural beauty of our scenery. Sendai Bay, with its hundreds of islets, has been famous since olden times as one of the three loveliest landscapes in Japan. The pines growing on these islets are 'Aiguromatsu', a natural hybrid between Japanese black pine (*Pinus thunbergii*) and Japanese red pine (*Pinus densiflora*), and they are famous both as picturesque full-sized trees and as bonsai. In the mountains around Sendai, we can collect Japanese white pine (*Pinus parviflora*) on the high slopes of Mounts Zo-o and Azuma, and in the lower mountain ranges we find trees such as cryptomeria, zelkova, and Sargent and needle junipers to transplant and train as bonsai. No matter whether they have chosen to grow bonsai from collected wild trees, from seeds, or from cuttings, the bonsai amateurs of Sendai have been inspired in their art by nature's majestic ocean and mountain scenes.

WHERE BONSAI GET THEIR START

For bonsai-minded visitors to Japan, Omiya's Bonsai Village is the most refined bonsai center of all Japan. It is there that the finest bonsai may be seen in commercial nurseries. It is a "must" place for bonsai fanciers. It may be called the bonsai showcase of Japan. But do not forget that bonsai must be raised from little plants, so visitors to Japan should also see one or more of the larger bonsai-raising centers that are scattered from the south to the north of Japan. In such centers, often in villages or suburban towns, numerous bonsai-raising families have been engaged in the specialized effort of raising bonsai from seedlings and cuttings. Their work extends to the trimming and training of bonsai. Many of these families live in Kurume City and suburbs in northern Kyushu, in Nagoya and vicinity, in Niigata in northwest Japan, and other areas—including Kinashi. Here, I tell briefly of Kinashi Village, now incorporated in the City of Takamatsu, where it is situated in the Seto Inland Sea National Park.

The history of raising bonsai in Kinashi goes back some three centuries, as it does also for most other large bonsai-raising centers. There are now no less than 200 bonsai-raising families in the Kinashi area, working exclusively on bonsai culture. Kinashi is renowned for Japanese black pine and white pine bonsai. If you were to walk around on a footpath between the rice fields you would find many nursery fields, with tens of thousands of Japanese white pine, one to several years old, grafted on Japanese black pine stocks. Footpaths extend for several tens of miles, and once I felt very sorry for members of the Brooklyn Botanic Garden staff who had come to visit the nurseries. They walked until they were exhausted.

Bonsai benches are seen everywhere in the front yards of bonsai-raisers' homes. They hold rows of Japanese black pines or white pines 10 to 100 years old, collected from their natural habitats, then greatly reduced in size by pruning. Such trees are handled in numbers throughout the village. To observe them in the different stages of their training never fails to arouse the interest of a visitor.

— K.Y.

Omiya:
Bonsai Showcase

In Bonsai Village in Omiya, Saitama Prefecture, Japan, there are two natural stone monuments. Both were erected in 1935 on the occasion of the tenth anniversary of the founding of this "bonsai town." Through their inscriptions they celebrate the achievements of the founder and his cooperators.

Engraved on one monument are two Chinese characters which represent the winning of immortal fame. The other bears an inscription telling how Bonsai Village was founded and how it also prospered. It relates how Mr. Shimizu, whose name had been Ritaro (proprietor of the Shimizu-en bonsai nursery), bonsaiman by trade, had prospered in Tokyo. As the Tokyo environs became unfavorable for bonsai growing after the earthquake and fires of 1923, Mr. Shimizu sought a new location that would be suitable in every way. He finally found such a place in the town of Omiya and moved there in March of 1925. He worked assiduously for years and with the cooperation and help of R. Suzuki, Tomekichi (the father of Mr. Saburo Kato whose contribution appears elsewhere in this handbook) and Katsuzo Nishimura, the bonsai town has prospered ever since.

No visitor to Japan should fail to visit Bonsai Village in Omiya. It is only one hour by rail from downtown Tokyo. — K.Y.

PHOTOGRAPH BY ELIZABETH SCHOLTZ

CASCADES

C ascade style has developed from the forms taken by trees hanging from a cliff. Just as these must be deep-rooted to withstand wind and storm, so a cascade is planted in a deeper container than most bonsai to anchor it and balance the composition."   *— Zeko Nakamura*

A cascade bonsai is one in which the main trunk and branches are trained to grow down over the edge of the container, giving the feeling of a tree jutting from a rocky ledge. A fine bonsai in this style usually has a sinuous, winding trunk which suggests the storm-tossed existence of its prototype. Its "clouds", or foliage masses, cluster around the trunk's outward bends. On the cascade's viewing side, a branch is often trained to grow partly across the front of the tall container in order to break the line.

As for plants to use in cascade training, many small-leaved species that are appropriate for upright styles also make pleasing cascades. One tree which lends itself to quick results is the weeping willow, whose flexible branches are easily wired into almost any position. Frequent pinching of the

new shoots and well-timed fertilizing should produce an attractive plant within one or two growing seasons. Weeping willows grow so rapidly, however, that they require frequent retraining to keep them graceful and in scale; and for this reason they cannot be used to make bonsai of distinction.

The traditional bonsai species—particularly small-leaved azaleas, junipers, and certain flowering and fruiting trees—are the best material for fine cascades. An attractive miniature cascade can be created with the Tom Thumb variety of rockspray (*Cotoneaster horizontalis*).

A tree which is to be trained as a cascade is usually planted at a slant in its container. Guy wires, fixed rather loosely at first and then tightened every few weeks, are often the initial training method used for bending the trunk downward past the container's edge. The serpentine curves into which the trunk is then trained are produced by traditional wiring techniques. The masses of foliage which should grow at outward bends of the trunk are created by frequent pinching of the new shoots to encourage profuse branching at these points.

THE PLEASURES

OF

COLOR

GEORGE F. HULL

One quality of bonsai that is often overlooked is color. We are likely to remember as an outstanding example of bonsai some weather-beaten juniper or twisted pine, an image in the mind of line and mass etched only in black and white. But this idea of monochrome can sometimes be carried too far. Color is part of nature, and it is in the area of color that I think many amateurs will find some of the early pleasures on the path toward bonsai. A few examples of colorful plants that have been grown by hobbyists in this country will indicate some of the possibilities.

One is flowering quince, a common shrub adapted to most areas, which is popular because its beautiful flowers stud the bare branches early in the year.

GEORGE F. HULL *is Garden Editor of the Chattanooga Times, Chattanooga, Tennessee. He is a"veteran" of bonsai classes at Brooklyn Botanic Garden, and author of* **Bonsai for Americans** *(Doubleday, 1964).*

Although old specimens respond well to drastic pruning of both top and roots, the quicker route to a flowering bonsai is to select a younger one with interesting branch structure from the wide assortment of container-grown plants offered by nurserymen. The dwarf Japanese quince (*Chaenomeles japonica* in variety) is one of several kinds that often assume picturesque branching when quite small. In late winter such a plant may be repotted into something more attractive than the nursery pot, the root ball made more shallow for better proportions, excess and crossing branches pruned away and, perhaps, one or two wired to a different position for better composition. The plant is ready for an early spring show. As soon as buds indicate the start of growth, the plant should be brought to a cool place indoors and kept watered. After flowering, keep the plant in good light and away from hard frost until spring weather has moderated to the point where it is safe to put it outdoors.

Continued on page 50

Above: *Cyrillia racemiflora*

At Left: 369-year old *Rhododendron indicum*, Satsuki azalea.

Developing an azalea of real bonsai stature might require a long search for a suitable old plant, and some skill and time in adapting it to the right container. On the other hand, enjoyment of azaleas in bloom can be immediate, even if their training as bonsai has just begun. Japanese connoisseurs grow some varieties of azaleas that remain models of restraint for eleven months of the year, then don a Mardi Gras cloak of brilliant color. For bloom in the true bonsai tradition, varieties with small flowers are appropriate. Azaleas by nature have shallow, compact root systems that permit safe transplanting even when they are in bloom, if reasonable care is exercised. In some climate zones, brilliant early-flowering azaleas can prove to be more rewarding as potted plants than when growing in the garden. At our home, where spring weather often produces rapid changes from hot sun to driving rain to frost during some seasons outdoors, the early azaleas may prove to be attractive five days or fewer. Indoors we regularly expect to enjoy the potted ones for five weeks.

Japanese maples are another example of a species whose color may be quickly enjoyed in a container. These are very slow-growing trees that take a long time to achieve enough size in the garden to make them effective, unless a very high price is paid for an old specimen. Small container plants, on the other hand, can be displayed so their beauty may be seen at close range and enjoyed despite their size. Even young nursery plants, especially some of the thread- or fern-leaf varieties (*Acer palmatum dissectum*) may be found that have developed picturesque forms. Spring foliage is colorful; some kinds remain red all summer, and most of them turn to beautiful shades of yellow, orange, and scarlet in autumn in climates where they are adapted.

A little plant hunting among the tropical or subtropical species can be productive of colorful plants. One that I have seen well grown is pistachio (not the one that produces the edible nuts, but a Chinese relative sometimes grown in California and other mild climates). The compound leaves turn brilliant orange and red before they drop. Malpighia is a tender evergreen shrub with tiny hollylike leaves used in Florida gardens, sometimes as a hedge. Older pot plants soon develop interesting trunks and exposed-root systems.

Traditional bonsai also offer color interest throughout the seasons, especially effective because of the close view such plants make possible. At this intimate approach we see the tiny bundles of yellow-green leaves on larch, the "candles" of new growth on pine, the winged fruits of maple. Many common trees have lovely flowers that are overlooked on large specimens. How often do we enjoy the beauty of flowers and budding leaves on oak trees?

Some of the plants mentioned here will never achieve the treelike proportions of venerable bonsai, but I believe their inclusion in American collections, for those who find them attractive, is justified in the same way that expert Japanese fanciers often show their sentimental attachment to some ornamental species, such as the fragrant fingered citron (*Citrus medica sacrodactylus*) or specimens of *Rohdea*. 🔖

PRUNING
FOR
BASIC FORM

In training bonsai from nursery-grown trees, it is important to remove all but the key branches. These will form the simplified skeleton of the bonsai-to-be, since it is from these limbs that new leaves and new shoots will grow. Foliage masses can be created around each branch if new shoots are pinched back as they develop.

In pruning the five-year-old tree **A**, only one branch is allowed to remain at

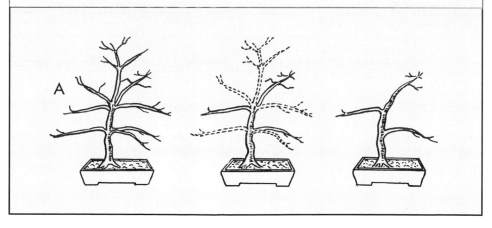

A

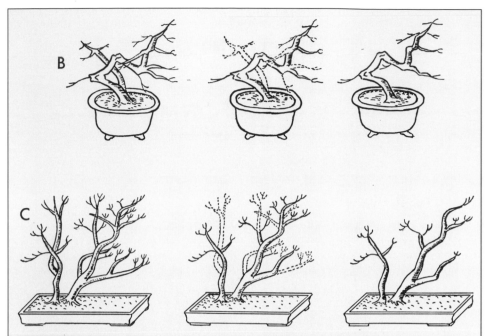

each level. This avoids the oversymmetrical effect of opposite branches, creates a feeling of openness between branches and accentuates the diminutive trunk. Tree **B**, a distorted specimen such as can occasionally be found in a nursery or growing wild, is pruned mainly to simplify the branch structure and emphasize its asymmetrical trunk. The trees in **C** are a kind one is sometimes fortunate enough to discover: specimens with interesting branch patterns, selectively pruned, are immediately attractive as bonsai.

PINCHING
TECHNIQUES

For Deciduous Trees

Beginning in early spring, pinch back throughout growing season. When a tree is growing vigorously, frequent pinching gives best results. In general, allow as many as five new leaves to develop on a young branch; then pinch back to the first one or two at top of tree, and the first three or four elsewhere (see drawing 1).

Choose a side bud that points in the direction you want a branch to grow, and pinch just above it. If buds grow in pairs, one of each pair should be removed to give plant a more asymmetrical appearance. Likewise remove alternate shoots, as in 2a and b.

Liquidambar orientalis, Oriental sweet gum, trained by John Naka.

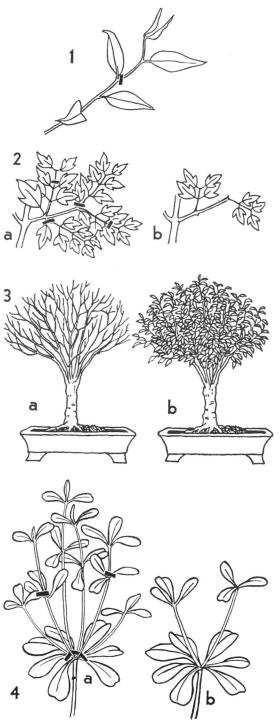

With healthy deciduous trees of some species, such as maple and zelkova, all the foliage can be nipped off in early summer, so that tree is completely bare (**3a**). A new crop of leaves, daintier in size and more decorative, will develop in a week or so (**3b**). See page 40 for Makoto Inawashiro's description of this procedure. Caution: Total leaf stripping is never practiced with needled evergreens.

For Flowering Trees and Fruit Trees

With flowering and fruiting trees, pinching is timed differently for different species so that incipient flower buds will be left intact. Azaleas, for example, should be pinched severely just after flowering. Of the five new shoots (**4a**) which usually appear, only one or two should be retained, and these should be cut back to two or three leaves (**4b**). Later in growing season, azaleas are pinched more sparingly so that some flower buds will form.

For Evergreens such as Juniper and Cryptomeria

With evergreens which produce new shoots throughout growing season, pinch

off a few tips more or less daily while tree
continues to send forth new growth. For
scale-leaved juniper, gradually remove
tips, as shown in **5**. When pinching
species with needled leaves (as in **6**), be
careful not to cut through needles which
are left on tree, for remaining stumps
will turn brown.

For Evergreens such as Pines, Spruces and Firs

With evergreens whose main growth oc-
curs in spring, pinch young shoots at that
season by removing half or more of each
just as individual needles begin to show.
Drawing **7** illustrates pinching of pine
"candles." See also Saburo Kato's description of pinching spruce (page 76).

Disbudding Pines

If needles of a pine bonsai become too
long in relation to size of tree, all buds
can be removed (as shown in **8**) approximately every third spring. The plant's appearance may be poor for a season, but
the new buds and the needles that come
from them the following season will be
much smaller.

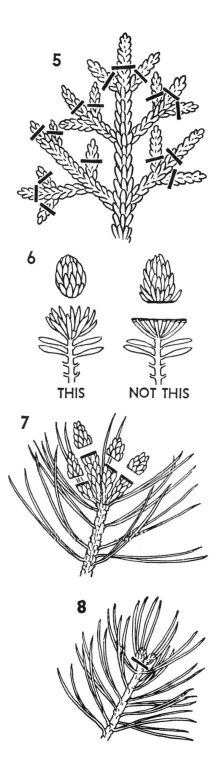

THIS   NOT THIS

BONSAI MINIATURES

ZEKO NAKAMURA

Cotoneaster horizontalis, four inches high, in BBG collection.

A finished bonsai is the result of long years of endurance and patience in caring for it and training it to grow in a container. Unlike a plant living in a garden or growing wild, its daily watering cannot be neglected. I am very busy working in the theater, movies and TV, but I manage to find time for watering my collection of miniature bonsai, and I do all the transplanting and training myself. When I have to be away from home all day, which happens often, my whole family is willing to help with the watering

Miniature bonsai are so small that they must be watered an average of three times a day, and five to seven times a day in summer. Also, each watering involves wetting the plants three times: the first soaks only the surface soil, the second penetrates to the middle of the containers, and the third wets all the soil so that surplus water runs out of the bottom holes. This incessant watering is the major drawback to miniature bonsai, an annoyance not only to the beginner but also to many connoisseurs. Beginners are likely to scant it and consequently to have their plants die.

ZEKO NAKAMURA *is a well-known actor in Japan, famous as a comedian and as a grower, trainer and connoisseur of miniature bonsai. He keeps his collection in the garden of his home in Tokyo.*

One of the great advantages of miniatures, on the other hand, is the small amount of space they occupy. Provided that it is sunny or only lightly shaded, a shelf or area about three by 7 feet is space enough to grow 100 to 200 plants. As I described in the Botanic Garden's first handbook on bonsai, for many years I kept a collection of about 400 on a shelf built on the roof of my house. Since then I have moved to a house with a small garden and have increased the number to 1,000. They now include almost all the Japanese woody plants that can be made into bonsai.

Nearly all my miniatures are four inches high or less; but even so, the crab apple, orange, pomegranate, peach, apricot, quince and chestnut trees bear fruit for me. The whole of last winter, for example, I enjoyed a four-inch crabapple bonsai hung with 25 scarlet apples. My only failure in fruit has been with Japanese persimmon, which, since it bears fruit as a regular-sized bonsai, I assume needs more root space than miniature containers provide.

Of the flowering trees, my collection is so varied that there is no month without flowers in my garden. Probably the most spectacular are 80 miniature Japanese cherries in a variety called 'Kyokuzan'. In the spring every plant is smothered with full-sized flowers, actually too big for four-inch trees. Last year I displayed some on a television program which featured Miss Cherry Blossom, who was visiting Japan from the United States. The response was almost too enthusiastic, as a large number of feminine televiewers then rushed to my house.

The person who wishes to learn how to raise miniature bonsai needs to know the common techniques for planting and taking care of them, together with some general principles of style and form used in their training. For miniatures, however, the maxim "Learn from the tree" is the main point about style: you need not be a slave to the rules. I myself interpret the traditional forms with considerable freedom, and the naturalness of my miniature bonsai was much praised in a three-man show I once gave together with a flower arranger and a ceramic artist.

My advice to the novice is to start by growing herbaceous plants in small containers, in order to get practical experience while using moderate-priced materials. I think the best way of all to begin is by attempting to dwarf wild flowers — dandelions, gentians, asters or any tiny small-flowered plants that are available in your locality. Besides helping you master the technical difficulties of miniature bonsai culture, these will give pleasure in themselves when they flower for you. As the grower acquires experience, in one way and another he will cause the death of many plants; but this everyone must accept, since it is inevitable in the course of learning how to grow bonsai.

Although I am no botanist, in the course of forty years' work with plants I have become more skillful in my hobby of miniature bonsai than in my profession as an actor. This is perhaps unfortunate for the profession, but good for the plants. Here are some suggestions out of my own bonsai experience that may save others from making mistakes.

WATERING. In spring and fall I water two or three times a day; in summer five times as a rule, but seven times on windy days. Winter winds in Tokyo are so drying that I put the bonsai in a coldframe, where they need water only once a day or every other day, provided I am careful about particular plants which dry out faster than the rest. Since the soil often freezes at night during midwinter, I water after ten in the morning, and never in the evening.

As described earlier, each of these waterings involves wetting the soil three times. Here in Tokyo, city water direct from the tap is irritating to the plants, so I put it in a large jar and let it stand before using.

SUN. As long as they are watered copiously, my miniatures do best when kept in full sun, even at midday. Those grown in the shade tend to be delicate, and their flowers are paler. For example, when a red-flowered plant is brought indoors for a week before it blooms, the flowers open pale pink or white.

Sunshine is good for people as well as for plants. Watering my bonsai has kept me in the sun so much that I am burnt almost black. I think this may be the reason I have not been ill in the past forty years.

SOIL. The kind of soil used for miniature bonsai is of the greatest importance; yet it is also a highly individual matter. I take the red or blackish clay with no organic content which is dug from deep underground, expose it to the sun for a week, and then sterilize and sieve it. However, miniature bonsai grow equally well in fine loam soil. The beginner should try out various soils; no better teacher than experience.

TRANSPLANTING. All potted plants become sick of their soil after a while, especially miniatures, which are growing in two or three spoonfuls. I repot most of mine annually, trimming one-third of the roots each time. Even pines, which are transplanted and root-pruned only about once in ten years when they are regular bonsai, require it every five years as miniatures.

Generally speaking, transplanting is done in the early spring just before the buds open. It is time to begin work when temperatures during the day average about 60 degrees. The procedure is the same as with regular bonsai, although for miniatures it is especially important to provide good drainage and to use screening over the bottom holes so that the soil will not be washed away.

Like a man just out of the hospital, the transplanted bonsai need careful treatment. The leaves of broad-leaved trees should be cut in half to reduce demands on the newly trimmed root system. The foliage of all varieties should be syringed daily, and protection should be given from sun and wind for a week before the trees are gradually moved back into the sun.

FERTILIZING. My recommendation is to be very sparing with fertilizer. Miniature bonsai are so small that they are easy to overfertilize, and this is often fatal to them. If necessary, they can utilize the nutrients already in the soil and grow normally for a year or so without fertilizer.

I use liquid fertilizers which are so highly diluted that the plants have no unpleasant smell when they are handled or brought indoors for appreciation. These liquids should be poured on only after watering. As for the best seasons to apply fertilizer, I begin in the late spring and continue weekly through the summer. During rainy periods, however, I stop using it, and I apply it only occasion-ally in winter. This schedule keeps the bonsai healthy at the same time that it helps in the dwarfing process. Growth is naturally vigorous in early spring and during rainy spells, and fertilizing then will simply overstimulate the plants.

Overfertilizing often causes the leaves to turn yellow or white, and to shrivel and die if it is severe enough. Japanese white pine is especially susceptible to this kind of damage.

DISINFECTION. Nowadays many kinds of gardening sprays are on the market. Follow the manufacturer's directions carefully, and spray the plants two or three times a month, including the undersides of the leaves. Use an old toothbrush to wash the trunks with the chemical, as insects, often invisible, may be embedded in the bark.

My favorite homemade spray is composed of cigarette butts steeped in water to which soap is added. The diluted liquid is effective for the less stubborn insects, and it is milder for the plants than garden sprays sometimes are.

TRAINING. Although the trunk and a few main branches of miniature bonsai are sometimes shaped with wire, by far the largest part of their training consists of scissors training. These plants are too small for much wiring, and it is better to be patient even though it takes more years — an average of ten, I would say — to produce a well-trained bonsai. Actually, I find scissors training so interesting that it is one of my chief pleasures in growing miniature bonsai.

There are a few other techniques I use in training miniatures. For example, it is my impression that broom-style *Zelkova serrata* develop more quickly if their branches are softly smoothed upward by hand whenever one has the time. Also, a

Miniature bonsai in the BBG collection.

trunk can be thickened artificially by "exercising" it several times a week — that is, by holding it at the bottom with one hand while bending it from side to side with the other. The resulting separation of the bark from the woody part causes a kind of "inflammation" which leads to thickening. Be careful, however; too-violent exercise can kill a tree.

MINIATURE FORESTS. As I said earlier, there is no need to follow traditional styles rigidly with miniature bonsai; often a design that is free and artless looks better than one shaped according to formula. As an example, here is a suggestion for creating a miniature forest without observing the rules and restrictions which make it such a difficult art in

bonsai design: Pick up a handful of small trees at random, set the whole handful down in a container, plant them wherever they happen to lie, and then rearrange some trunks or branches slightly with tweezers. Such an offhand arrangement sometimes has a naturalness and simplicity that cannot be duplicated by artifice. If, on the other hand, you wish to follow a ground plan in making a miniature forest, try the design I have sketched in drawing 1 (page 61). Notice that the container should be shallow and open; the secret is to leave space within it in order to suggest the sweep of a natural landscape.

STONE-CLASPING MINIATURES. As shown in drawing **2**, I make this kind of planting by placing a miniature tree into sticky clay which I have smeared in the hollow of a stone. The tree can be anchored into position with wires which have already been fixed to the rock, as in the first sketch of the drawing (see Seizan Ito's instructions for attaching wires to a stone, page 25). This kind of planting is not exposed immediately to full sun; the tree takes a while to become established on the rock and should be kept in a shady spot protected from wind.

CASCADES. Cascade style has developed from the forms taken by trees hanging from a cliff. Just as these must be deep-rooted to withstand wind and storm, so a cascade is planted in a deeper container than most bonsai to anchor it and balance the composition. Cascading miniatures are started with well-grown trees that are two or three years old. Before wiring a tree, I sketch several possible cascade designs and choose the best among them. Don't change your mind about the shape after you have wired a cascade; beginning over again will only damage the tree.

SOURCES OF PLANTS. Like regular bonsai, miniatures can be grown from cuttings or seeds, can be collected as wild plants and can be propagated by air layering.

I take cuttings from a plant by slicing off small branches, using a sharp knife and making slanting cuts. I remove the tips of these slanting ends, as shown in drawing **3**, and insert the cuttings deeply at a slant into a suitable rooting medium which contains no fertilizer. I water them copiously, set them in semi-shade out of the wind and spray the leaves from time to time. I find that early spring when the buds are bursting is the best season for growing cuttings. It seems as if almost everything except bamboo can be propagated by this method; many growers even

1

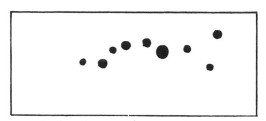

Ground plan for a miniature forest. The container should be shallow, and open space should be left around the trees to suggest the sweep of a natural landscape.

2

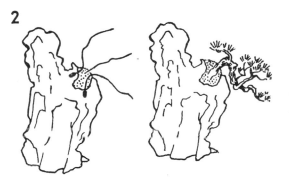

Planting a stone-clasping miniature in the hollow of a rock. Copper wires are attached to the stone, and the hollow is filled with soil. After the tree is planted, the wires are wrapped around it to anchor it securely. Then the soil and wires can be concealed with a layer of moss.

3

Propagating miniatures from cuttings: Insert them deeply at a slant into a suitable rooting medium with good drainage.

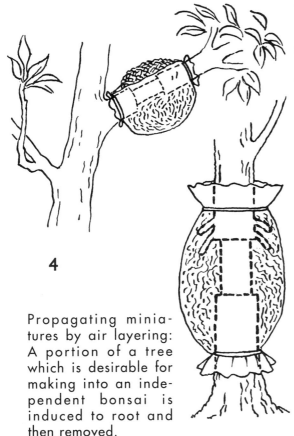

4

Propagating miniatures by air layering: A portion of a tree which is desirable for making into an independent bonsai is induced to root and then removed.

use it to raise pines.

To grow miniature bonsai from seeds, I sow the seeds in early spring in the same kind of soil used for cuttings. I keep the seedlings in flats for a year, occasionally giving them weak fertilizer, and transplant them to single containers in the second year.

Of wild plants collected from the mountains, four- and five-year-old seedlings are best for training as miniatures. Most of my bonsai shown in the photographs are plants I collected when on location making movies. After I find a suitable small plant, I dig it up carefully, trying not to damage any fibrous roots but removing the taproot. I leave some soil attached to the roots, wrap them in moistened moss or newspaper and carry the trees home in plastic bags. For the first year I plant them in a larger pot than the usual bonsai container. Although collecting is most successful in the spring when the wild trees are just beginning to sprout, they can also be dug up at other times of the year, especially if one takes them home with a fair amount of soil attached to the roots and gives them extra care at first.

In air layering, a portion of a tree which is desirable to make into an independent bonsai is induced to root and is then removed. Early summer when the tree is growing most actively is the best time for this. As shown in drawing **4**, the bark is removed over an area two to two and a half times the diameter of the branch, and the wound is covered with well-moistened sphagnum moss or fine soil, which is then bound in place with a sheet of plastic loosely fastened at the top for frequent watering. In a month and a half, new roots will have developed, and in two months the branch is ready to be cut off and planted separately.

Air layering is a well-known technique the world over, and varies in detail only according to the kind of plant that is being aerial-rooted. The pomegranate I have shown in drawing **4** illustrates a typical procedure for deciduous plants.

In closing, I should say that all my rules for taking care of miniature bonsai may not work for you. As every collector's plants become accustomed to the environment he provides, they develop different requirements. One person's miniature bonsai, for example, may do very well when watered only twice a day; another's may die if not watered six times. When you have mastered the principles behind the rules, you will know what your plants need, and they will repay your care by growing their best, bearing flowers in the spring and fruit in the fall and so giving you joy in return.

WATERING BONSAI

In the spring, water evergreens and deciduous bonsai once each day, preferably in the morning. In the summer, water bonsai two or three times each day depending on the amount of sunshine and wind as well as the depth of the container. Watch them carefully.

In the fall, on sunny days, water bonsai once a day, in the morning. During long periods of cloudy days, less water is required. Watch carefully, and when water is needed, give it in the morning.

In the winter, water once daily on sunny days, in the morning. Watch carefully during long periods of cloudy days, and when water is needed, give it in the morning.

The technique is this: Water from above with a spray that does not disturb the surface soil. Continue watering until water is dripping through the holes in the bottom of the container.

Another method for watering is to submerge the lower three-fourths of the container in a tub of water and allow it to remain there until the surface of the soil looks moist, or about 20 minutes. This requires a bit of labor if one's bonsai collection is large.

Frequently, the surface of the soil will appear to be moist, so it is best to scratch it with fingernails or a stick to determine the need for additional water.

—FROM LYNN R. PERRY, *BONSAI: TREES AND SHRUBS, A GUIDE TO THE METHODS OF KYUZO MURATA.* COPYRIGHT © 1964. THE RONALD PRESS COMPANY, NEW YORK.

COLLECTING A MOUNTAIN AZALEA

SHINICHI SHIBAZAKI

Rhododendron kiusianum from Kyushu, southern Japan,

must be potted in sand, protected from lace bug,

trained by pinching rather than wiring.

Although several areas in Kyushu have wild plants suitable for bonsai culture, the two great mountain ranges on the island are especially well known for the many species they contain. At its high point the Mt. Yufu range is slightly more than 5,000 feet, while the Mt. Kuju range rises to almost 6,000. Beginning midway up these slopes grow such plants as Japanese white pine (*Pinus parviflora*), *Rhododendron metternichii, Enkianthus campanulatus longilobus* and, most famous of all, Kirishima mountain azalea (*Rhododendron kiusianum*).

Today most bonsai of *R. kiusianum* are

SHINICHI SHIBAZAKI *is Executive Vice-President of the Oita (Japan) Sake Brewing Company; a veteran collector of wild trees for bonsai.*

started from cuttings, for the tree grows wild only in this vicinity, and Mt. Yufu and Mt. Kuju have been made national parks. But although plants can no longer be taken from their slopes, wild specimens of this mountain azalea can still be found in the hilly country near the big ranges. The plant is collected during its dormant period from November to March.

The most important step in adapting *R. kiusianum* to container cultivation is to remove all the mountain soil from the roots. If any is inadvertently included in the container, it seems to cause the roots to rot and the plant to die in two or three years. The only soil we use for these azaleas when they are grown as bonsai is a volcanic sand, which provides perfect drainage. In transplanting a wild tree, a few strands of moistened sphagnum moss

are placed around the roots to encourage growth of a dense root ball. Because of the shock to the roots as a result of removing all soil, a collected plant does better if its branches are cut back in order to reduce demands on the root system.

Kirishima mountain azalea flowers in the spring, different varieties producing crimson, pink, purplish pink and white blossoms. The white-blooming kind is rare and costly; the crimson comes next in value.

As soon as flowering is ended, the old flower parts should be cut off to prevent seeding, which weakens the plant. In the climate of Kyushu there is no need for winter protection, as these trees are high-mountain residents.

The lace bug is very fond of *R. kiusianum* and quickly gathers on the underside of its leaves, turning them yellow and killing the branches. It is easily controlled, however, by spraying the plant once a month with malathion.

Unlike most other bonsai, this mountain azalea does not adapt well to wiring. Training is carried out by pinching or by tying branches with string, for any wire wrapped around them is likely to cause their death. *R. kiusianum* grows well on a stone, either by itself or as the secondary planting with a stone-clasping pine.

Three or four years are required to train a collected specimen, while it takes seven or eight years for *R. kiusianum* raised from a cutting to achieve a tasteful appearance. When the training period is over, however, this tiny-leaved and delicate-flowered azalea is a bonsai which its owner will be proud to display. 🪴

MY GARDEN IN YAWATA

Minoru Minashu

As I awaken in the morning, my feet carry me almost without thought to the garden, where my beloved plants are awaiting me. Laden with morning dew and displaying the colors of the season, my bonsai are lined up on their shelves. The exquisitely small features of *Rhododendron kiusianum* are so charming that I stop some minutes to look at them. The strong exposed roots of a Japanese white pine appear more impressive every day. Each plant, though humble in quality, brings me pleasant memories of its training, and I pass the time with them forgetting things in everyday life.

The streets of Yawata, where I live, are full of foul air, as there are so many facto-

Minoru Minashu *of the Yawata (Japan) Iron-works is Secretary of the Yawata Ironworks Garden Club.*

ries. Yet by taking pains, many of us are able to grow bonsai perfectly. Some find space for their bonsai shelves on the rooftop of an apartment house, while others keep them in a small garden like mine.

Every bonsai grower in Yawata has his favorite type of plant for bonsai; mine is *R. kiusianum*, long a celebrated species in Japan, which is coming to have world-wide popularity. Also called Kirishima mountain azalea, it is native only to the high mountains of our southernmost Kyushu, one of the four main islands which make up Japan. When a specimen has been collected from the wilds, training is commonly begun by cutting it back severely, often to the bare trunk. New shoots which then sprout are trained to form a thick new crown lower on the trunk than the old one. Today, however, *R. kiusianum* is usually propagated from cuttings. Within three years after a cutting is rooted, it is two to three inches high and has begun to flower in the spring. Most blossoms of this dwarf azalea are various shades of pink, though some rare kinds have white flowers.

In training bonsai, I enjoy making cascades and stone-clasping plantings. To create a cascade I start with a plant such as the cotoneaster I have sketched in skeleton form in the first drawing above. I transfer it to a tall container and wire-train its trunk and branches into the curves shown in the second drawing at right. From its best viewing angle, a cascade should grow downward to one side or the other in order not to hide the container.

For stone-clasping bonsai I often use pumice stone, since it is soft enough to work with a chisel or knife. By this means I make the bottom concave so that the planting will be completely stable. Then I chip a hole in the stone as shown at **A** of the drawing at left and score two grooves (**B**) down its face. I line the hole and grooves with sticky soil and set the tree in the hole, leading the roots along the grooves down to the soil in the container. Finally I cover the roots with sphagnum moss which I fasten to the rock with strings.

After I work for a time with my bonsai in the morning, I go to my job at the Yawata Ironworks, which employs 40,000 people. In my spare hours I am secretary of the Ironworks garden club, consisting of about 250 employees who are interested in bonsai, ornamental plants and landscape gardening. We have arranged many trips to bonsai nurseries, and also to potteries which manufacture bonsai containers. Our affection for bonsai creates a strong bond between the members, and we are peaceful among ourselves from living with nature as a friend. 🌺

Cotoneaster before and after being shaped into a cascade bonsai.

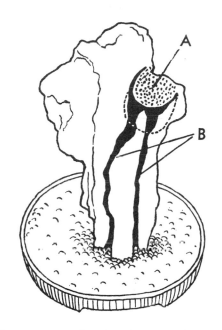

For a stone-clasping bonsai: A cavity is chiseled in a soft pumice stone at A, and grooves (B) are scored down the face. A and B are lined with sticky soil, the tree is set into A, and its roots are led along grooves down to soil in the container.

67

WIRING TECHNIQUES

"**N**ever be in a hurry.... It is the hands which must do the learning, slowly and repeatedly until they can think for you."   —*Yashiroda*

Pinus thunbergii, Japanese black pine, 22 years old.

Wiring has two purposes: to help the tree attain its ideal form, and to correct overlapping branches so that all can receive the sun and evening dew.

—Saburo Kato

Pinus thunbergii, cultivar, cork bark black pine, 39 years old.

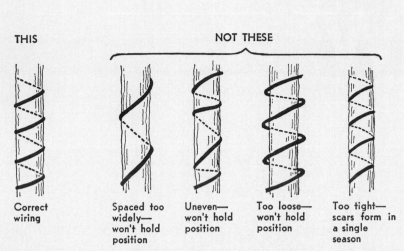

THIS	NOT THESE			
Correct wiring	Spaced too widely— won't hold position	Uneven— won't hold position	Too loose— won't hold position	Too tight— scars form in a single season

Use no. 10 to no. 26 copper wire, depending on branch thickness and stiffness. Soften larger-size wires by bringing to a red heat in a flame and letting cool gradually. Once coiled around a branch, softened wire soon hardens.

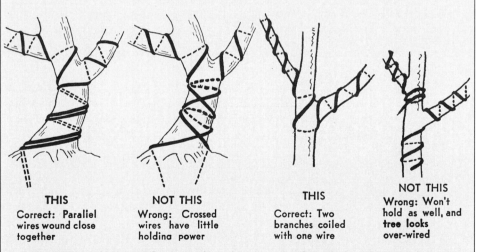

THIS	NOT THIS	THIS	NOT THIS
Correct: Parallel wires wound close together	Wrong: Crossed wires have little holding power	Correct: Two branches coiled with one wire	Wrong: Won't hold as well, and tree looks over-wired

Begin wiring at bottom of tree and work upward. If trunk is to be wired, anchor wire ends by pushing down through root ball to a bottom corner of container. Avoid sheathing a tree in wire; good wiring practices give best results with least wiring.

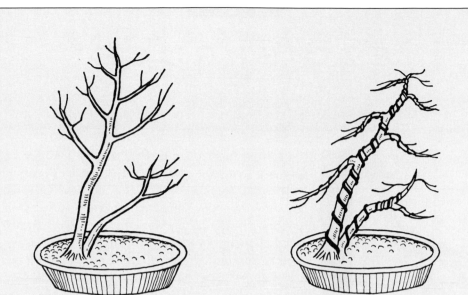

Branches growing upward can be trained to slope downward or outward, suggesting the form of an aged tree.

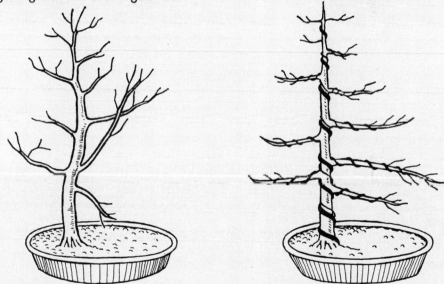

Wind wire clockwise for training a branch to the right, counterclockwise for training it to the left. Wire should be of a size just stiff enough to hold newly bent branch in position.

DRAWINGS ADAPTED FROM TOSHIO KAWAMOTO AND JOSEPH Y. KURIHARA, *BONSAI-SAIKEI*.

EZO SPRUCE*

SABURO KATO

f you travel in Japan someday, you will find that Ezo spruce (*Picea jezoensis*) is one of the most popular trees for training as bonsai. Public demand for spruce has increased many times over since new varieties with rare and delicate beauty were discovered on Kunashiri Island about forty years ago. Though Kunashiri is very close to Hokkaido (formerly called Ezo), its forest contained spruce of exquisite forms and characters that had never been seen in Hokkaido. Kunashiri Island was then a national park and its forest protected by law, but the governor of that territory, who was a bonsai fancier, allowed bonsaimen to collect specimens of naturally dwarfed Ezo spruce growing wild in the park. Soon these became a favorite throughout Japan. In 1945 Kunashiri, which is a part of the Kuril island chain, was occupied by the Russians and its forest closed to bonsai collectors. Some fine cultivated varieties have been developed from the original wild strains, however, and a tremendous number are propagated each year. This article on their training consists of excerpts from my book *Ezo Spruce, and Forest and Stone-Clasping Bonsai*, reproduced by the kind permission of the publisher Kashima Shoten.

Pruning

Every tree has its own way of growing, and the basic pruning which gives it shape as a bonsai should reflect this as well as expressing an ideal form. While the grower plans the design he wants the tree to have, he should be carefully observing its individual character and habits of growth to see whether his ideas are truly suited to it.

For this reason I recommend that pruning be done not all at once, but over a few years as one watches the tree's reaction to his work. A plant pruned too quickly and forced into a preconceived pattern is likely to have its natural growth

SABURO KATO *is proprietor of Mansei-en Bonsai Nursery, Bonsai Village, Omiya, Saitama Prefecture, Japan. He is President of the Bonsai Association of Japan.*

*Although called Yeddo spruce in America, this name is erroneous. In Japan it is called Ezo Matsu, after its habitat Ezo — which is the island now called Hokkaido. Yeddo is the old name for Tokyo.

Picea jezoensis, Ezo spruce.

impaired. Some people, for example, are led by the plan they have formed beforehand into pruning back a weak branch, which then often dies and spoils the design. The grower who waits to develop a sense of the tree's own ways will learn to encourage the weak branches to produce denser foliage, while he cuts back the vigorous ones to keep them in scale. This slow and gentle approach to pruning is easier for the grower and kinder to the plant, and I find that it produces the best results. While gradually leading a bonsai toward the shape one has in mind and at the same time pleasing the tree, one can achieve the ideal pruning.

Wiring

Wiring has two purposes: to help the plant attain its ideal form, and to correct overlapping branches so that all can receive the sun and evening dew. Thus I think it is a mistake to look at a wired tree as a persecuted plant; it is good for the tree to have a good result in the future.

Of course, one must be careful not to

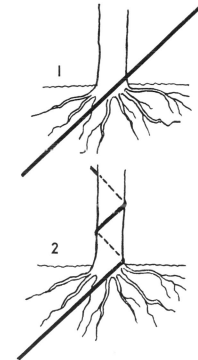

1 & 2: In wiring the trunk, it is important to anchor the wire properly in the soil.

73

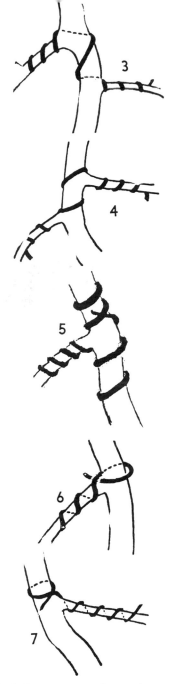

3 & 4: Wiring two branches with one wire. 5: Anchoring a wire under the main wire which is coiled up the trunk. 6 & 7: Anchoring a wire under its own loop.

harm the tree in wiring it. Use copper wire in sizes ranging from no. 10 to no. 22, and soften the larger sizes by bringing them to a red heat (as explained on page 70). The two best times for wiring Ezo spruce are in the early spring and late autumn. However, a newly transplanted tree should not be wired for a year. If a cold spell comes in the autumn when a tree has just been wired, it should be kept under shelter.

As with pruning, one should study the tree thoroughly before wiring it. Plan the shape which is best for the design and best for the tree's growth; then decide the basic procedure of wiring. If the trunk is to be wired, wiring should start at the bottom as shown in drawings 1 and 2, with a long piece of the wire-end anchored in the soil as closely as possible to the trunk. In wiring a branch, it is more effective to use a wire which connects two branches, as in 3 and 4. But if this is impractical, a single branch can be wired by anchoring the wire-end under the heavier wire that has already been coiled up the trunk, as in sketch 5, or by

74

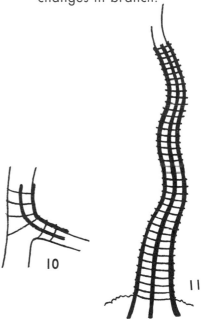

8: Wire coils spaced for slight changes in shape of branch.
9: Wire coils spaced for drastic changes in branch.

fixing the end under its own loop, as in **6** and **7**.

Wire is coiled with the loops spaced according to the purpose of the wiring. The spacing shown in drawing **8** is suitable for lowering a branch somewhat or curving it slightly. But to put undulating curves into a straight branch, or to straighten a naturally crooked one, the loops must be closer together, as in **9**.

A most effective device is to combine coiled wire with wires running parallel to the branch. For example, this device may be useful with a limb which seems in danger of breaking if it is curved to slant downward by means of ordinary wire coiling. As drawing **10** shows, two rather heavy wires are bent into the shape the branch is to take, and these are lashed to the trunk and to the top of the branch with coiled wire. Braced in this manner, the limb is far less likely to fracture. A much thinner wire can be used for this type of coiling than would be necessary without the parallel wires.

As drawing **11** shows, the same general technique can be applied to an

10 & 11: Coiled wire combined with parallel wire braces.

Pinch by taking the end of a new
shoot between the tips of forefinger
and thumb and pulling it off.

entire tree trunk, except that the parallel wires are placed all around it instead of only at the area of strain. In this situation it is an advantage that thinner wire can be substituted for the large and unwieldy sizes usually necessary for shaping a trunk. Another advantage of this method is that wiring scars are slow to form. By keeping the coiled wire away from the trunk, the parallel braces prevent injury to the bark even when the wire is left on for two or three years.

Some bonsai experts use only one or two heavy guiding wires, and bind the trunk to them with strong cord.

Except in special circumstances, wire coiling is begun on the lowest branch and proceeds upward to the highest. Some bonsaimen prefer to finish all the wiring on a branch before moving up to the next, while others do the main wiring on all branches before they go back and wire the smaller twigs at the tips.

Pinching

The new clear green needles of Ezo spruce which sprout and grow in the spring are so beautiful against the dark older foliage that they may almost be thought of as its flowers. The buds of Ezo spruce bonsai do not open simultaneously but in order of size, starting with the largest. It takes two weeks to a month for them all to burst, so pinching is begun with the earliest and is continued over a period of weeks. It seems a pity to pinch off such lovely buds; but if it is not done, the dormant buds will not sprout, growth will be untidy and the tree will become unkempt.

How is Ezo spruce pinched? The right time has passed when the new growth is fully developed; pinching should take place when the buds are only half sprouted. It is then quite easy to pinch them back by taking the end of a shoot between the tips of the forefinger and thumb and removing it as if pulling it off. If it is sliced off with a fingernail, some of the needles which remain on the tree are damaged and will turn an unsightly brown. After very little practice, anyone can become expert.

How far back should the shoots be

pinched? This depends on many factors — the density of the old growth behind the shoot; the requirements of the design; the length of time the tree has been in the container. Although the thickness and length of Ezo spruce needles vary from tree to tree, they can be controlled to some extent by several pinching methods. In general, one-third to one-half of a new sprout should be removed. The deeper the pinching, the thinner the new growth; the lighter the pinching, the denser the new growth. In a part of the tree where very thick foliage is desired, the new shoots can be left untouched.

When an Ezo spruce has been established in a container for years and is well shaped as a bonsai, it should be pinched back severely in order to preserve its form. Also, it will produce shorter needles if the new shoots are pinched earlier than the half-sprouted stage described above. Earlier the pinching, shorter the needles. In fact, if the needles are becoming too long and altogether untidy, the buds can be snipped off before they have begun to open. The growth from the next season's buds will be very much shorter and neater. Such drastic treatment should be limited to healthy and vigorous trees, however, and even then should not be done more often than every third year.

Propagation

Ezo spruce is usually propagated by taking cuttings from the two- or three-year-old branches of a vigorous tree. The most favorable season is early spring before buds have sprouted. The customary way is to cut the twig on the slant with a sharp knife, remove the needles from the bottom of the cutting and push it at a slight angle into the rooting medium for one-third its length. If the cuttings are very small, they are inserted with tweezers.

The soil is then lightly pressed, and the cuttings are watered with a fine spray. The boxes of cuttings should be placed where they receive evening dew but are sheltered from sun and wind. For a month they are syringed three or four times a

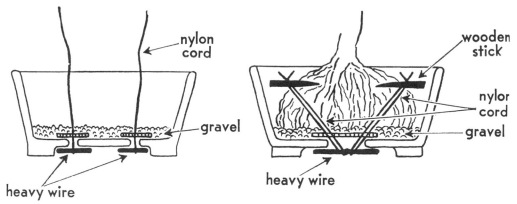

Two-hole container: Tree can be tied in position with nylon cord.

One-hole container: Tree can be anchored with sticks tied to nylon cord.

day, and the soil is prevented from becoming too dry or too wet. After this, the cuttings are syringed twice a day for two months; then they are gradually exposed to full sun, starting with an hour a day.

Watering

Since bonsai are grown in a limited amount of soil, and since most are kept outside in the sun and wind, plentiful watering is very important. For bonsai which stay indoors away from direct sunlight, it is not easy to judge how much water they need. A general rule is to water them sparingly every day and copiously every third day. In winter, indoor bonsai are usually drier than one imagines and should be watered generously. I never saw any bonsai that died in the winter from root decay due to overwatering, but I know of many that died from drought.

Fertilizing

Ezo spruces are fond of fertilizer, but they should not be given much at a time. Older trees are fertilized only once a month in their growing periods during the spring and fall; young trees can be given fertilizer twice a month in those seasons. Transplanted trees should not be fertilized for at least a month, however.

Transplanting

Generally, spruce trees are transplanted every third or fourth year, although a tree in a large container can often be left for six or seven years. The best season is in very early spring before the buds have expanded; other times are in the fall and in the winter after the weather has turned cold. It should never be done in late spring when the buds are opening.

To transplant a spruce bonsai, tap the ball of earth out of the container and remove some soil with a chopstick. Starting with the bottom of the earth ball and then moving to the sides, take away half the soil for a young tree or one-third for an older tree. Examine the exposed roots carefully; use a sharp knife in cutting away decayed and damaged parts and pruning back some of the longer dominant roots.

Before repotting, prepare the container: Tie nylon cord to a short piece of heavy wire, cover the drainage hole with plastic screening and thread the cord through the screen. The drawings illustrate some ways to do this for a container with two holes and for a container with one hole. When there is one hole, the nylon cord can be tied to two short sticks which are thrust into the root ball as an anchor. There are many variations of these methods (for example, see page 25 in the Botanic Garden's Handbook on Bonsai: Dwarfed Potted Trees); everyone will be able to develop his own.

As with all bonsai, a layer of gravel is put on the bottom of the container for drainage, and a layer of new soil is spread over it. After the tree is set in and anchored into position, new dry soil is added and worked around the roots with a chopstick. Finally, the surface is covered with either moss or ornamental sand [Americans may substitute parakeet gravel — Ed.]. The tree should be watered thoroughly so that water runs out through the drainage holes, and its foliage should be sprayed too.

Bonsai, which are created through our passion to express the varied beauty of nature artistically, require much technique to attain complete harmony between a container or stone and a plant. Besides, we must promote the strength of a plant to grow for itself, and must particularly respect its originality. If we always love and cultivate a bonsai, it will reveal its own nobility and personality as the years pass. The height of its beauty, shown according to the change of every season, gives us a deep impression and rest of mind.

TRAINING BONSAI: FIRST STEPS. . .

PROCEDURE BY FRANK OKAMURA

Start with this five-year-old Japanese holly *(Ilex crenata helleri)*.
Moisten, ball and wrap the root system of the freshly dug plant.

. . USING A NURSERY-GROWN PLANT

PHOTOGRAPHS BY ROBERT S. TOMSON

Study the branch structure, and prune away all but the key branches. Leave only those which are essential to the future character of the tree.

Dominant roots should be cut well back. Stiff, straight branches are given more graceful lines by wiring (see pages 68 to 71 for techniques).

Root ball is much reduced in order to fit container. The two containers above illustrate steps in positioning pieces of screen over drain holes, inserting wire which will hold plant in container, and adding gravel for drainage. Foliage masses will develop in a single growing season from the basic "skeleton" shown here.

Kan Yashiroda training *Pseudolarix amabilis*, golden larch, in 1955.

PHOTOGRAPH BY FRANCES M. MINER

STORY OF
A GOLDEN LARCH

Pseudolarix amabilis.
Same golden larch 35 years later in 1990.

BONSAI SHOULD BE WATCHED WITH CONSTANT AFFECTION

Bonsai is the art of planting a tree in a container, and growing it as a healthy plant by giving it enough care so as to be able to enjoy a miniature replica of graceful natural scenery. So it is important to watch over one's bonsai with unfailing affection. Any person who wishes to grow bonsai should spare at least ten to twenty minutes every day, either in the morning or the evening. Without such effort, successful bonsai growing can hardly be expected.

And if one has a true affection for his bonsai, he cannot fail to take notice of the drying of the soil in the container, the condition of the buds, color of the leaves and growth of the new shoots (which determines the amount of fertilizer to be given), the infestation by insects or disease, condition of the flowers and fruits, withering of the leaves, decay of the roots, etc. Upon finding defects, countermeasures must immediately be taken.

ADAPTED FROM KYUZO MURATA, BONSAI: *MINIATURE POTTED TREES* (SHUFUNOTOMO CO., LTD.)

ABOUT TRUNKS

LYNN R. PERRY

If you take two bonsai of like material and age (for example, two maples that are five years old which have been trained as bonsai from seedlings, cuttings, layerings, or nursery stock) and plant one in the container and one in the ground, the one in the ground will increase in trunk diameter over a period of two or three years much more rapidly than the one in the container, which may show little or no increase.

Both trees are treated as bonsai, are root-pruned at the proper time, top-pruned throughout the growing season as required, watered, and fertilized on like schedules. The tree in the ground may need to be root-pruned again during the growing season. This is done by cutting around the root system with a spade and lifting it in order to halt the development of a tap root in species which have this type of root system. It is set back in the hole immediately. It may require less watering because its 'container' is much larger and does not dry out so rapidly. It may be wired in the nursery row if desired.

The disadvantage of growing bonsai in the nursery row is that the trees are not in their containers and in their place in the grower's collection. However, the advantages to be gained by using this means of thickening the trunk of the bonsai are worthwhile. If the grower can wait as long as five years while the bonsai grows in the nursery row and is trained there — particularly root-pruned — fine specimens can be developed in a short period.

LYNN R. PERRY *lived in Japan for some years and studied bonsai with Kyuzo Murata at the Kyuka-en Bonsai Garden. She was on the staff of the Botanic Garden in 1963, and is now proprietor of the Suzu-en Bonsai Company, Erie, Pennsylvania. Teacher of bonsai culture, lecturer, and author of* **Bonsai: Trees and Shrubs — A Guide to the Methods of Kyuzo Murata** *(Ronald Press, 1964).*

LYNN R. PERRY, BONSAI: TREES AND SHRUBS — A GUIDE TO THE METHODS OF KYUZO MURATA. COPYRIGHT © 1964, THE RONALD PRESS COMPANY, NEW YORK.

Juniperus occidentalis, Sierra juniper, 309 years old.

Carpinus Tschonoskii showing trunk detail.

BONSAI SOIL MIXTURES

GEORGE F. HULL

The separate mineral elements that make up natural soils range from sand, the coarsest, to clay, the finest. Clay is so fine (particles below .002 millimeter) that water will penetrate it at a rate of only one foot a day, while sand (.05 to 1 millimeter) is so porous water will pass through 1500 feet of it in the same time. As might be expected, sand dries out quickly, while clay hangs onto moisture for a long time. Roots grow well in sand, if frequently supplied with the right amount of moisture, which accounts for the generous use of sand in mixtures for seedlings and cuttings. Roots find compact clay inhospitable, so grow slowly in it or perish, if it is poorly drained.

It is unusual to find either clay or sand in pure deposits. Natural soils are mixtures of materials of many sizes, created by such actions as the settling of moving water as silt, deposits by the winds as loess, the accumulations of organic matter and minerals on forest floors, or the result of many other forces. These mixtures, which range somewhere between pure sand and pure clay, we call loam.

Loam is a combination of many-size particles. If most of these are very fine, it is called a clay loam. If of a medium-fine size, a silt loam. If coarse, a sandy loam.

The granular texture of a soil is not dependent entirely on the size of the mineral particles. Even clay soils, if properly treated — in "good tilth." as the farmer would say — have a granular structure, due to the fact that fine particles of clay form small clumps, with spaces between for the movement of air and water. The roots of plants require both air and water, and a good soil has a high percentage of air-water space in relation to its solid elements.

We usually think of loam as containing humus, a product of decaying vegetation and other organic matter. This organic substance adds to the fertility of the soil, soaks up large quantities of water, thereby making a sandy soil more moisture retentive; it increases porosity, thereby making a clay loam more open

to the penetration of air, water, and roots. Humus sounds like the panacea for all soil ills, but used in high concentrations or alone, it is not. Gardeners have found that, under certain climatic conditions, organic materials like peat moss or peat humus alternately can stay too wet too long, and then when dry, become actually water repellent.

The ideal soil would have the good qualities of the extremes — the structural porosity of sand, the water-retaining ability of clay — without the undesirable fast-drying characteristic of the former, or the inhospitable density of the latter. If we could create such a soil, and add the right amount of humus, then presto, we would have the perfect potting soil. It sounds magical and unattainable, but the Japanese have gone a long way toward attaining this ideal. How? By following two practices that are not generally known in this country.

First, they sieve their potting soils, retaining several granular sizes and — especially in the case of clay soils — they throw away the finest part. Second, they pot with dry soil. The theory is that the inclusion of the dusty part of fine soil will fill up pore space, and that damp potting soil containing clay will lose much of its porosity if firmly packed into the pot. Dry soil can be tamped around the roots without destroying its granular structure. The tiny granules of clay act as reservoirs of moisture, and between them are the air-water spaces and the other materials of the potting mixture, the sand and humus.

All successful bonsai growers in this country do not follow these practices, but if clay soils are used, it is indicated. In cool, humid areas, where droughts are infrequent, moisture-retentive soil is not so important. And, of course, if watering is attended to frequently enough, a fairly light soil will serve almost anywhere. 🌲

FROM *Bonsai for Americans*, by George F. Hull. Copyright © 1964 by George F. Hull. Reprinted by permission of Doubleday & Company, Inc.

PREPARATION OF SOIL FOR BONSAI

Screening Procedures at Brooklyn Botanic Garden

A	B	C	D	E
Soil which remains on top of 1/4" screen	Soil which remains on top of 1/8" screen	Soil which remains on top of 1/16" screen	Soil which remains on top of 1/32" screen	Soil which posses through 1/32" screen

A & B mixed for DRAINAGE at bottom of pot

C & D mixed in equal parts LOAM MIXTURE*

*The clay content of the loam determines its water-holding capacity.

DIRECTIONS FOR MAKING AVERAGE POTTING MIXTURE

LOAM MIXTURE 3 parts	+	SAND or PERLITE 1 or 2 parts	+	LEAFMOLD or PEAT MOSS 1 part	+	MANURE (Bovung) 1/2 part	+	BONE-MEAL 1/2 part	=	FINAL POTTING MIXTURE

ACIDITY OR ALKALINITY OF BONSAI SOIL

Determinations of the pH (degree of acidity or alkalinity) of soils in which many kinds of bonsai grow successfully have shown a range of 4.5 to 6.5. Since pH 7.0 is the neutral point, a slightly acid condition is obviously best.

In general, acid-loving plants such as rhododendrons and azaleas do well within a pH range of 4.5 to 5.5. Pines and other needle-bearing trees normally grow in soils with pH 5 to 6. Indeed, most deciduous species that are used for bonsai (maple, hawthorn, flowering quince, pomegranate, cotoneaster, etc.) do well in the same 5 to 6 pH range.

If potting soil for a bonsai is taken from a place where similar plants are growing, there should never be a pH problem.

If necessary to make soil of a particular bonsai specimen more alkaline, add a light sprinkling of lime to the surface of the soil. To make it more acid, add a light sprinkling of sulfur.

The soil in the bonsai container is the total environment for the tree's roots. This needs to be maintained in top condition.

SOIL CONDITIONERS

LYNN R. PERRY

Bonsai growers are generally aware of the importance of air as well as water in the soil of bonsai containers. The health of a bonsai depends on the presence of both, and both should move rapidly through the soil. If water lies on the surface and seeps but slowly into the soil mixture, it is a good indication that the mixture is too tight, i.e., soil aeration is poor. In some areas where soil tends to be "face-powder-fine," the problem of soil aeration and drainage in a bonsai container calls for special attention.

93

In Japan, bonsai soil mixtures usually include volcanic soil or sand, since it holds several times its own weight in water and generally promotes the growth of roots. Soils of volcanic origin are difficult to find in the United States except on the West Coast or Hawaii.

I have recently become acquainted with a soil conditioner called "Terra-Green," and another with the name "Turface" (available in regular and coarse grades; the regular is also available with nutrients added, and is sold under the trade name "Support"). These are clay, which is screened and baked. Because the clay has been baked, the particles are very hard and their shape cannot be changed. I find that when one of these soil conditioners is used as a sand substitute together with local soils, it is possible to go back to the recommended Japanese mixtures and have much the same results as if I were using soil of volcanic origin. For conifers I use 6 parts Terra-Green or coarse Turface and 4 parts soil. I use 6 parts soil and 4 parts of a conditioner for all other bonsai except when potting ericaceous plants. Then it is necessary to add 3 or 4 parts screened peat moss to the 6 parts soil and 4 parts conditioner. This reduces the number of potting mixtures in my nursery to three.

The results are almost immediately apparent. Excess moisture cannot remain in the soil; therefore bonsai plants cannot "drown." A smaller, finer system of roots forms rapidly. I also note that moss grows more rapidly on surfaces of soil mixtures which include the conditioners described. Turface is manufactured by Wyandotte Chemicals Corporation, Wyandotte, Michigan, and Terra-Green by the Oil-Dri Corporation of America, Chicago. Both are available in many garden and department stores.

BONSAI ON A ROCK

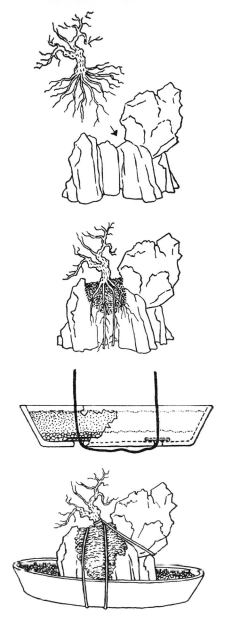

T he goal of planting a bonsai on a rock is to reproduce, in miniature, the natural appearance of a tree growing on a boulder or on a small rocky island in the sea. Plant in early spring just before the buds burst forth with new growth. Small-leaved maples and low-growing junipers are well suited for this type of bonsai.

SELECT A SUITABLE ROCK, attractive in shape, age-weathered in appearance, and stable (that is, flat or essentially so) on the bottom. A saddlelike depression with miniature valleys descending from it is ideal.

PLANTING TREE ON ROCK. Take a picturesque tree with well-developed roots and wash them free of soil. A thick coating of a mixture of clay and peat moss should be smeared on the rock where the roots are to grow. Divide the roots into three or four bunches, and position the tree on the rock so that it appears as natural and graceful as possible. String, raffia or stout rubber bands may be used to hold the base of the trunk firmly in place.

DISTRIBUTING THE ROOTS. Train the roots down the cracks or grooves in the rock, making them cling by applying more of the mixture of peat moss and clay. Add a few strands of sphagnum moss, placing them in contact with the roots, and fasten everything to the rock firmly with rubber bands, raffia or string.

PREPARING THE CONTAINER. Place screens over drain holes, and add gravel and soil as for growing any bonsai. Wires running through drain holes will fasten rock and tree as a unit firmly in the container. Or after planting, string or raffia may be tied around rock and the outside of the container to hold them securely.

WATERING. Spray frequently with enough water to keep roots continually moist until they have grown down to the soil of the container. After this, treat the plant as you would any bonsai. For repotting instructions, see Seizan Ito's article on Stone-Clasping Bonsai.

—ADAPTED WITH MODIFICATIONS FROM KYUZO MURATA'S *BONSAI: MINIATURE POTTED TREES* (SHUFUNOTOMO CO., LTD., TOKYO).

CARE OF BONSAI IN WINTER

KAN YASHIRODA

Hardy plants are those that can live outdoors in the coldest weather without danger of winter-killing. They are **not** house plants but are real outdoor plants. Typical examples are many kinds of pine, spruce, yew, retinospora (*Chamaecyparis* species), hemlock, cedar, larch, holly, maple, privet, flowering crabapple, hawthorn, rockspray, etc. These plants need cold to remain healthy and grow well. But be cautious!

Hardy species growing in bonsai containers present a special problem if left outdoors in below-freezing winter weather. Soil in the containers will freeze, and the containers will often break. Moreover, it is impossible to properly water bonsai growing in firmly frozen soil.

If a sunporch or cold but light room is available where the night temperature never falls below about 36 degrees F, this would provide a good place for overwintering hardy or semi-hardy bonsai.

Another suggestion is to keep the plants in a deep coldframe that is insulated. It should be shaded by a lath house. The soil in bonsai pots, with such protection, should never freeze if the night temperatures do not go much below 0 degrees F. The bonsai should be watered as needed, and on warmer nonfreezing winter days, it is well to remove the protective covering and give the plants full air. Be sure to replace the covering sash before sunset.

If no garden space is available for such a coldframe, a large insulated wooden box might be constructed on a terrace. Its cover should be the same as for a coldframe. Soil in the box can be kept from freezing by the use of electric cable.

Many nonhardy or tender species trained as bonsai will grow satisfactorily if treated as house plants. Typical plants in this group are tender azalea, camellia, gardenia, box, dwarf pomegranate, firethorn and rosemary.

Sectional view of deep coldframe suitable for the winter storage of bonsai in cold climates. The frame should be situated in shaded area completely free of winter sun (lath house shade is satisfactory). Plastic covered sash on top should fit tightly. As many as 30 plants can be stored in a 5- by 6-foot frame.

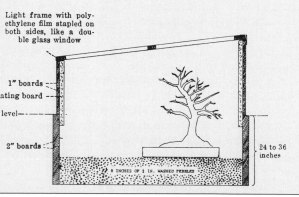

Light frame with poly-ethylene film stapled on both sides, like a double glass window

1" boards
1" insulating board
Ground level
2" boards
24 to 36 inches
8 INCHES OF ¼ IN. WASHED PEBBLES

Watch our garden grow in your very own mailbox!

From Great Neck to Great Bend, Big River to Little Creek, over 20,000 people in all 50 states enjoy the bountiful benefits of membership in the **Brooklyn Botanic Garden** – including our renowned gardening publications.

Brooklyn Botanic Garden Membership

The splendor that makes the Brooklyn Botanic Garden one of the finest in the world can be a regular part of your life. BBG membership brings you subscriptions to some of the liveliest, best-researched, and most practical gardening publications anywhere – including the next entries in our acclaimed 21st-Century Gardening Series (currently published quarterly). BBG publications are written by expert gardeners and horticulturists, and have won prestigious *Quill and Trowel* awards for excellence in garden publishing.

SUBSCRIBER $35

(Library and Institution Rate $60)

* A full year of *21st-Century Gardening Series* handbooks
* A year's subscription to *Plants & Gardens News*
* Offerings of Signature Seeds, handbooks and videos
* Reciprocal privileges at botanical gardens across the country

Plants & Gardens News – practical tips and suggestions from BBG experts.

FAMILY/DUAL $50

All benefits of SUBSCRIBER, plus

* Membership card for free admission for two adult members and their children under 16
* 10% discount at the Terrace Cafe & Garden Gift Shop
* Free parking for four visits
* Discounts on classes, trips and tours

SIGNATURE $125

All benefits of FAMILY, plus

* Your choice of a Signature Plant from our annual catalog of rare and unique shrubs, perennials and house plants
* 12 free parking passes
* A special BBG gift calendar

BBG Catalog – quarterly listing of classes, workshops and tours in the U. and abroad, all at a discount.

SPONSOR $300

All benefits of SIGNATURE, plus

* Your choice of <u>two</u> Signature Plants
* Four complimentary one-time guest passes
* 24 free parking passes
* Invitations to special receptions

GARDENING BOOKS FOR THE NEXT CENTURY

Brooklyn Botanic Garden's 21st-Century Gardening Series explore frontiers of ecological gardening - offering practical, step-by-step tips on creating environmentally sensitive and beautiful gardens for the 1990s and the new century.

Spring 1998
Please send in this form or contact BBG
for current membership information, higher levels and benefits.

21st-Century Gardening Series – the ne handbooks in this acclaimed library.